CLOSELY WATCHED STOCKS IN TOPEKA, KANSAS

WRITTEN BY

JOHN MICHAEL LEGG

TOTALLY INSPIRED BY

MOLLY MARGARET MURPHY

NEWMAN SPRINGS PUBLISHING
320 Broad Street
Red Bank, NJ 07701

First originally published by Newman Springs Publishing 2021

ISBN 978-1-63881-012-4 (Paperback)
ISBN 978-1-63881-013-1 (Digital)

Printed in the United States of America

Dedicated to all of those who are
trying to gain their sobriety.

John Michael Legg

CONTENTS

ACKNOWLEDGEMENTS AND SPECIAL THANKS TO:

- Susan Murphy
- Pastor Holmes and the Wannamaker Woods Congregation
- Stormont Vail Hospital doctors and nurses
- Valley Hope Rehabilitation Center in Atchinson, Kansas
- Alcoholics Anonymous (AA)
- Shane Jones

CHAPTER 1

INTRODUCTION

My name is Jayber Harland Sherrer. My friends and clients call me "Jay" for short. I've been a stockbroker in Topeka, Kansas, for Mayweather & Co. Inc. for the past thirty-four years. It's 6:30 a.m. and I'm at my desk at the office. I'm trying to find stock, bond, or option ideas that fit my clients' investment objectives. Being a stockbroker is what I wanted to do when I went to college, and I've been doing it for the past thirty-four years. When I was in college, I used to hang around this brokerage house in Topeka and watch, with great fascination, the stock quotes moving by on the electronic quote board mounted on the wall. I now work for that same brokerage firm. I thought then and I still do now that I literally was in the Candy Store, and that was where I wanted to be for the rest of my life. It took me ten years after college and Vietnam to get a job in "the Candy Store", and I'm still anxious to get to the office early in the morning every day. In the last few years, to my chagrin, they quit calling us "stockbrokers." They now refer to us as "financial advisors," and my employers are very insistent on that too. Nowhere in any company memos, and we get a lot of those, do they ever refer to us as stockbrokers. In fact, I've even heard my branch manager refer to me as just a "stock jockey." I didn't know whether to laugh or cry when I heard that. I thought he may have missed the greatest attraction we have for most of the people who come through our doors: the stock market. They want us to plug people into a network of money managers whom we have no way of really knowing what they might do. I would rather do the money management myself. Well, either way, I'm now sixty-seven years old, and I know I can't change, and I wouldn't if I could.

Even though I'm sixty-seven years old, I don't think of myself as being that old. I still walk with the same gait as I did when I was thirty years younger, and I can still work a twelve-hour day and not feel too tired to play most of the night with my ten kitty cats at home. Lately, however, I've noticed that young ladies often go ahead of me in the building where I work, and open the door for me and say something like "Let me help you with the door, sir." At first, I thought that there was some old man walking behind me whom they were referring to, but eventually I realized they were talking to me. Another one of those "laugh or cry items." Back to the office at 6:30 a.m. I'm usually looking forward to finishing my initial preparation for the market elsewhere, so at about 7:30 a.m., I often walk about a block away to a small cafe for breakfast. I go there armed with the *Wall Street Journal* and some other financial papers to read. The food is usually good, but the real reason I've been going there lately has nothing to do with the *Journal* or the food. There are usually three waitress working every morning, so I have a one-in-three chance of being waited on by a young lady who is a waitress there whom I've grown very fond of.

When I used to shave in the mornings, I would look in the mirror and remind myself of three things: First, there is a difference between "THE DEAL AND THE REAL DEAL." For me this has to do mostly with picking out the right investment. "THE REAL DEAL" often comes along six months after I think I've found the right deal. I know I need to be patient and study more till the "THE REAL DEAL" presents itself. Secondly, I remind myself of a saying we all know and I didn't invent, but applies to everyone at some time or the other: "A FOOL AND HIS MONEY ARE SOON PARTED." I know that one has applied to me a lot more than I would like to admit. And finally, rule three, "THERE'S NO FOOL LIKE AN OLD FOOL." This, of course, has to do with old guys like me chasing after much younger gals—something I didn't invent either, and many other guys have gone before me and will come along after me on that one. This amount of introspection got too much for me. So the only thing I could do is quit shaving and grow a beard and let my barber trim it every week. I just stay away from the mirror.

Over the past ten years, since my ex-wife remarried, I thought I had quit violating rule three, but like they say, "Hope springs eternal," and I find myself getting those ideas again. The girl I'm focused on doesn't open doors for me or call me sir. She talks to me and treats me like I'm still the guy I think I am. At the café, our conversations get longer and longer and sometimes she gets in trouble with her boss over talking to me too much. When I'm around her, time stops and for the first time; the market doesn't seem all that important to me. I know I've got it bad.

CHAPTER 2
MY APPROACH TO THE MARKET

It is now 8:30 a.m. CST, and the US markets are opening. I am usually putting in orders that I had stored up after last night's close. I'm the production leader of the broker team I belong to, and I'm very aware that I need to lead. In the morning, I try to have "jacks or better" to open the day. By now, I've had at least two hours to try to figure out the trend of the market for that particular day and what I think may happen, at least for the next few hours. I call it figuring out "who's on first" as it relates to the market. I remind myself that first-hour trading can easily make a fool out of even the best of traders. At any given time, I usually have built up fairly large positions in between ten to fifteen different stocks I have studied over a long period of time. When I'm dealing with a client that takes my advice, I try to produce at least a 25-percent annualized gain in normal markets. In fact, sometimes after I do really well on a deal, I'll jokingly ask our phone receptionist if Warren Buffett might have called for me. The answer is always no. In truth, I wouldn't leave here anyway, and as everybody knows, Warren does not need my help. He's the best and always has been. I'll have to settle for being a close second.

Sometimes I let the kind of day we are having on the market or on one of my stocks determine what I am going to do. One of my favorite stocks is Ford Motor Co., and it's down today, making an opportunity for many of my clients that already own it to add more shares. Or for those who don't own it, to start a position. Ford Motor Company, and all of the smart things their management is doing to advance their product is a great American success story I love to tell people about. When I research a company that I think I might be interested in bringing to the attention of my clients, I always look at the top management. Ford's management is one of the best. They planned ahead, and when things got really bad in the economy and the auto industry, they didn't go bankrupt like General Motor or Chrysler. Ford executed their plan and improved their company and their market position. For me to get on the phone and talk to my clients about the latest things Ford is doing is not hard. I often start moving into a stock before their "success story" is complete—that's so my clients will pay less for the stock, and they can afford to buy more shares. Ford's chart pattern is improving daily as well. I feel that the reason my clients benefit more from dealing with me is that they know I'm looking for stocks like Ford to bring to their attention. I started buying Ford stock for some of my clients at around $1.50 a share three years ago, and it's now even more of a bargain at $12.50 today. With a big dividend too.

Early this morning, I decided I would challenge myself to add at least ten thousand more shares of Ford stock to an already large total position my clients own. To make it interesting, I also decided I would not have lunch till I get it done. My main partner is eighty-three years old, and I believe he is still the best "lunch man" in the business. I'll let him handle lunch. I never wanted to be anywhere, but in "the Candy Store" during market hours. It isn't quite as serious as I may be making it out. When I'm talking to many of my clients, I often kid around, and I hope they enjoy the conversation even if they don't buy my recommendation that day. I'm sure, if my superiors in New York could hear me, they would wonder what to do with me. I am in a serious money business, but I never want to take myself too seriously. So, if I have an opportunity to bring laughter to the conversation, I will do it.

One of my first calls of the day is an incoming call from a lady I have known for a long time. This lady has worked for the phone company for over thirty years, and her retirement is very secure. I have a lot of fun kidding with her. The call goes like this:

"What's happening to Delta today? It's down almost a half of a point!" she yells frantically.

My response is, "It could be that article today in the *Wall Street Journal* saying some airlines could go bankrupt," knowing that that comment would set her off even more.

"Bankrupt!" she cries out. "I thought you said Delta was doing really well!" she pleads.

"Maybe I got it wrong. Come to think of it, they were not talking about Delta, they were talking about some other airline," I responded, acting somewhat confused. "Oh well," I add, "this is your money we're talking about not mine."

Then she threatens, "I'll take my account to Joe '[one of the other brokers in the office] if you don't straighten up."

I respond, "Joe is a really good broker, but you'll have to go to the golf course to find him."

I then tell her, "Try to be more patient. You've only owned Delta a few weeks, and you're already up three points. Besides, if anything big happens to Delta, you'll be the tenth person I call."

"What do you mean, tenth person?" she questions strongly.

"Well," I explain, "you have the tenth largest position that my clients have, and I should call the other larger holders first, don't you think?"

"That's just terrible," she says.

"What about this?" I go on to say, "you bring more money in, and we can buy you more Delta, and you can move up on the list and I can call you sooner. How's that sound?"

"I don't know what I should do with you," she says bewilderedly.

"Hey, I'm going to have to get off the line because I got someone waiting on the other line that says he has new money now. Okay?"

"I never," she says.

"Call me back when you get new money," I say as we hang up.

It's during this time I often initiate a call to a retired doctor client who is not just a client but a really good friend. He is very knowledgeable, well-read, and has lots of market savvy. He is well-versed in different types of market instruments we can use within his large accounts to best take advantage of a stock or market index we want to go after. The call today is about using what's called a "Bull Put/Call Option spread" to make a play on Ford Motor Company, which has been moving higher lately. This allows us to take a "bullish" position on Ford without putting in new money. What you need is a large account with plenty of margin capacity. The phone call might go like this:

"Good morning, Doc. I thought I might talk to you before you got off to the golf course today."

"You must have read my mind, I was about to call you. What's up?" he replies.

"You know, that 'Put/Call' spread we talked about yesterday is moving into position price-wise. Do you want me to nail it?"

"Let's do it," he responds. "Do one hundred options each side," he adds (that's a play on ten thousand shares of stock).

"Consider it done and you have a good game," I say.

I immediately do the trades while the prices are right. I sell one hundred "Put" options and then I use the proceeds to buy one hundred "Call" options. If everything goes as we planned, and stocks moves higher, the "Put" option obligation goes to nothing, while on the flip side, the "Calls" appreciate in price. Before the "Calls" expire, we sell the "Calls" for a profit or exercise the "Calls" and buy the stock at a discount. I love doing deals that cost my clients virtually nothing, and, if we are right, they can make a lot of money. Like I always say, "That's how the West was won."

CHAPTER 3

JUNE HAZEL BURNS

I'm not sure if I'm losing my focus or if my lifelong fascination with the stock market is waning, but I know something in my life is different. I think that something is June Hazel Burn: age twenty-four, friendly, intelligent, and a very pretty brunette.

One morning, as usual, I'm over at the restaurant where she works, pretending that I'm studying the *Wall Street Journal*, hoping June will be my waitress. This particular morning, I'm really lucky—she is. We start talking and I try to say something funny, not serious. At that time, we had not been out on a date or really alone together.

During the course of our conversation, June told me, "Jay, I need to start looking for an apartment of my own. Living with my mother isn't working out for either of us. I'm sometimes out late bar-hopping with my friends, and when I come in, it wakes her up."

At that time, I said something that was very surprising, even to me, because I had lived alone for a long time and I am a very private person. I never thought that, except for my kitty cats, I would live with anyone again the rest of my life—whatever was left of it. I blurted out, "I have a large house with extra rooms and a bathroom. Why don't you come live with me rent-free? You could save some money that way to help pay off your student loans," I added.

My self-control had left the building, and I had revealed myself to her. This was not our normal conversation. At that moment, I was having a little trouble catching my breath. My dad told me long ago that, in any negotiation, the person who speaks first after the initial pitch loses.

To redeem myself, I said, "You know, when I was your age, I wanted to get out on my own too." I guess I was afraid June would turn me down flat, so I gave her a way to gracefully decline my offer. She continued looking at me for, what seemed to be, a long time. I think she may have been a little amazed I offered that, since up till that point I had been a somewhat reserved person. I would like to think that she might well have been considering my offer.

I won't know because we both heard a bell dinging loudly; my order and other people's breakfast orders were ready to be picked up by June, and the cook wanted her to get the food and serve it before it got cold. "Jay, I've got to get everyone's food out to them, so I'll talk to you later," June blurted out.

Things seemed a little different between us after that. When we looked at each other, we often had trouble stopping. After a few weeks, June told me, "Jay, I've moved into a really nice one-bedroom basement apartment that is a good deal, because utilities are included and I'll be out on my own and I can come and go when I like."

"I would love to see your new place sometime," I responded.

We didn't speak again, at least for some time, about my offer. But my offer to let June move in with me did take us to a more serious level.

CHAPTER 4

NEW APARTMENT FOR JUNE

June told me, while we were talking at the restaurant, "I don't drive." She went on to say, "A few years ago my license was revoked after I had a DUI." She added, "My dad has been taking me to work most of the time, and when he can't, I try to catch the bus. One of the other waitresses that gets off when I do often drives me home."

"The state of Kansas is very hard on people that commit DUI's," I chimed in.

"You're sure right about that!" June responded. "There is a ton of stuff a person has to do to get their license back, and I just don't have the money for it now," June went on to say.

"June, I've been one of the lucky ones that never got stopped. There has been at least a hundred times in the past forty-five years I could have gotten a DUI myself," I added. "In fact," I went on to say, "When my ex-wife moved out of town, I started limiting myself to no more than two drinks before I got home because, if I were to get a DUI, I had no one else in town that could care for my kitty cats while I was in jail."

"June," I asked, "where do you live?"

She answered with the directions.

"Hey, gal, you are right on my way to work," I added. "Anytime your dad can't make it, I'll gladly pick you up because I'm headed that way about that time anyway." At that time, I wrote my home phone number on a scrap of paper and handed it to June.

She took the paper, but she didn't commit that she would actually call me. June had to get back to waiting on other tables at that time, so I headed back to work.

A few weeks later, at about 6:30 a.m. on a Friday morning, I got a call from June. "Is that ride to work offer still good for today, Jay?" June asked.

"Certainly it is," I responded.

"I can be there in about thirty minutes, is that alright for you, June?"

"It works for me. I'll see you then," she responded.

It started that Friday, and I was already hoping for more chances to pick her up soon. When June got in the car, she said, "My dad has his church early-morning prayer breakfast on Fridays. It's clear across town and he can't make it back in time to get me to work. Do you think we could make this a regular thing every Friday, Jay?"

"Certainly," I responded. Even though it wasn't much to go on, I felt our relationship had reached a new level, and, at least once a week (usually Friday mornings), I would get to talk to June maybe ten minutes while we were alone together instead of in a crowded café. That time would prove to be extra special to me.

On occasion, I was early, and she would let me in while she finished getting ready in her bathroom. June told me,

"Jay, make yourself comfortable on the couch. I'll be ready in a few minutes." While waiting for her in the living room, I noticed a sizable bookcase with a library of mostly classic books and DVDs. On her kitchen table, she had a craft project she was working on too. Often, when I talked to June at the restaurant, she would quote me verbatim lines from some of these books, so I knew she read a lot. I also noticed in her kitchen area a rather large trash container, usually full of 1.75-liter vodka bottles. This seemed out of place for the girl I had been talking to a lot lately.

June had a cat named Moxie. I had several cats of my own. It suddenly occurred to me that, other than our cats to keep us company, June and I were two lonely people living alone. I had lived alone for some time now and thought it would probably be forever, but I suddenly hoped it would not be June's fate too. She is a very pretty girl with lots of great things about her.

One morning at the restaurant, June was waiting for me, and she seemed somewhat bewildered. Looking back on it, we had been talking to each other now for almost six months and not really going anywhere with anything. June blurted out, with a hurt look on her face, "Why haven't you asked me out?"

This took me by surprise, and for a moment I couldn't speak. It had not occurred to me that June would want to take our relationship to a higher level—a level I had given up on a long time ago. We looked at each other intensely for what seemed like a long time. I knew I needed to speak next, and I knew what I said needed to be phrased right.

"June," I said, "Do you realize that I am almost six-ty-eight years old, and you are just twenty-five? And to make matters worse, I had a serious stomach operation a few years ago that was followed by four small strokes."

"Jay," June answered, "That doesn't matter to me at all."

We kept looking at each other as if no one else was in the place. This is one of those moments in life I felt that I just couldn't let get away or make light of.

"June," I repeated, "are you really sure it doesn't matter?"

She came back again, "Jay, it really doesn't matter to me."

"Okay." I seized the opportunity and asked, "What night this week would you be free to go to dinner?"

She did not hesitate and said, "How does tomorrow night at around 6 p.m. sound?"

"Sounds good," I responded. "I would like to take you to my favorite dining place in Lawrence, Kansas, at the old Eldridge Hotel. I haven't been there for a while, but their food and atmosphere is great."

June shot back, "Jay, I'll be ready at six tomorrow night."

CHAPTER 5

FIRST DATE

As first dates go, this one started out good, even though I hadn't been on a date for a while. I took off early from work to do some extra primping but left myself plenty of time to drive the fifteen minutes it takes from my house to June's apartment. I was later to learn that June skipped her normal after-work nap to do extra makeup and stuff to get ready too. I arrived promptly at 6 p.m. and pushed the doorbell to June's apartment. She answered the bell looking prettier than ever. Up until that time, I had never seen June in anything but her work clothes.

"June," I said, "you look absolutely beautiful in that dress you're wearing."

"Thanks Jay, you're looking great too," she responded.

With those pleasantries out of the way, we were in the car and on our way for the thirty-minute drive to Lawrence, Kansas.

My favorite place to dine out was, and still is, an almost century-and-a-half old hotel in Lawrence called the Eldridge. The food and service there is great in the very quaint nineteenth-century atmosphere. I hadn't been there much lately, because I hadn't had anyone to take, and I didn't want to make the trip just to dine alone. The place was just like it always had been in the past.

When we got there, I told June, "I've got to go to the bathroom, how about you?"

"Me too, Jay," June responded.

"Then follow me, June. The bathrooms are just off the lobby. I'll wait for you by the fireplace," I added.

When June got out, I took her hand and led her over to the large fireplace because I wanted her to see the portrait of Colonel Eldridge and his family. "June, in the late 1800s, when QuanTrill and his raiders sacked Lawrence, they burned down this hotel. It was Colonel Eldridge and his brothers who came to Lawrence from Kansas City and over the next few years rebuilt this really beautiful hotel, pretty much as you see it now," I told her while pointing to his portrait.

"Jay," June said, "I really appreciate knowing the history behind the place."

I then took June's hand and led her to the dining room.

During dinner, we were waited on by a very sharp young man whom I thought was likely a student at nearby Kansas University. I asked our waiter if he was a student at KU, and he responded that he sure was and hoped to graduate in two years.

June added, "When I was a student at Seattle Pacific University, I had about six close girlfriends, and we all had various jobs to help pay the bills. We shared the same apartment and studied together and sometimes shared the same boyfriends. At least once a year, we try to get together for a week somewhere."

"June, I think it is great that you are doing that. When I got out of Vietnam, I couldn't get a stockbroker job and worked for my dad in the heating and air-conditioning business for ten years. Since things were slow in the winter, I often took my vacations then and went skiing in Vale, Colorado. I had two buddies when I was in high school that had married and they and their wives moved to Denver, Colorado. On my way to Vale, I stopped to see them every year. After I married, I took my new wife to Vale, but she didn't like skiing, so I never went again. When we divorced, I pretty much quit going out altogether and didn't go to any of the high school reunions either. I hope you continue to keep up with your friends. I think it's important."

After dinner and an after-dinner drink, I asked June, "Why don't we stroll down the street a few blocks and look at some of the shops to see if there might be something we could get to remember the date by?"

"Jay, I'm not going to let you spend a lot of money on me. The dinner was pretty expensive, and that's enough," June responded.

June didn't know I had brought an extra five-hundred dollars with me in case we found something she liked. As I would find out later, June was hard to buy for. She already had plenty of clothes and kitchen items, and a hope chest full of everything else.

It was still only about 9 p.m., but I knew June had to be at her job early the next morning, and I could see her head dropping down a few times.

"June, why don't we call it a day? After all, we both have to be at work early tomorrow morning."

"That sounds good to me, Jay. I hope you don't mind?"

When we got to the car, I started back for Topeka as fast as possible. June immediately fell soundly asleep. She slept so hard, I had trouble getting her awake when we reached her apartment. She did finally awake, and gave me a quick kiss on the cheek, thanked me for the evening, and disappeared into her apartment. As I pulled away to head home, I thought I hadn't impressed her, and this date would probably be one and done. I probably wouldn't get a second date. Sleep didn't come easy for me, regardless of how many sleeping pills I took to try to get the evening out of my mind.

Up early the next day, it just so happened it was my morning to pick up June. I was very apprehensive as I approached her apartment, because I didn't know how she would act. I got to her place about 7:15 a.m. June was waiting for me outside on a bench in front of her apartment. She got in the car, leaned over, and gave me a big kiss and said, "Let's go out again soon, Jay!"

All my worries began to fade away, and it looked like I was going to get a chance to try again soon. GREAT!

CHAPTER 6

SECOND DATE

I quit trying to get a second date years ago. I usually didn't get the first date, so getting a second date seemed unexpected. But June herself said, "Let's go out again soon." That was a statement that stuck with me.

So the next time I saw June, I said, "Since you are only getting one day off a week, why don't we go out on a night you can sleep late the next morning?"

June quickly responded, "That sounds like a good plan to me, Jay." June went on to say, "I'm off next Tuesday, so how about we go out that Monday night?"

I did not hesitate to say, "That works for me, so it's a date, and I'll plan to pick you up at 6:30 sharp next Monday night."

Since it was still only Thursday, the days drudged on slowly. When 6:30 Monday night rolled around, I was at June's doorstep to pick her up. When we got in the car, I said, "June, would you like to go to Olive Garden tonight?"

"Sure, Jay," June responded. So off we went.

During dinner, since June had never been to my house, I said, "Would you like to go to my house after we finish here?"

"That sounds great," June responded.

Since it was cold out that night, and I had a large fireplace, I went on to say, "I've got logs in the fireplace ready to light too." My house, at that time, was over thirty-five years old. While I had been gradually fixing it up, it was in need of a lot of work. Still, it was spacious, and set up on a well-landscaped yard, with lots of kitty cats peeking out of the bushes.

June said, "Jay, you have told me that you have several kitties. I would like to meet them."

"Well, sweetheart, you are headed for the right place because, as of this moment, I have ten kitties at or around my place," I said. "Plus," I went on to say, "after I finish breakfast every morning at the café where you work, I feed at least six more kitties on the two block walk down an alley on my way to the building I work at."

"I would love to see them too sometime soon, Jay," June added.

When we arrived at my house, I gave June a quick tour.

"Jay," June said, "this house has all sorts of possibilities."

"I'm sure it does, but I'm here all alone, and the outdoors is a lot of work, especially since the front of the house yard is over three hundred and fifty feet wide with lots of trees and scrubs to care for. And the back is spacious too. I have a hard time keeping up, but I do have someone come in twice a month and clean," I added.

I wasted no time getting a fire going in the fireplace, which takes up almost a whole wall in the living room. Soon we had a roaring fire going. June and I got some pillows and cushions from the nearby sofas and put them on the floor to lay on. Several of the cats were starting to come out to see June. I introduced them to her.

"Sweetheart, these are my four guys. There's Rocky, Robbie, Rambo, and Rex, and their mother, Little Star." Also, not to be outdone, two other kitties were peeking at us over the banister on the second floor. "June, up there is Dee Dee and Dangerous Dan looking down at us. I'm not sure where the others are right now"

"Jay, this place and all your kitties are really awesome. I'm thinking we need to come up with a name for your home. What do you think?"

"June, you're good with words, so why don't you work on that?"

"I will," June responded.

I then hurried to the kitchen and pulled a chilled bottle of champagne out of the refrigerator, got two glasses, popped the cork, and poured some for us both. That old house hadn't seen much in the way of romance for years, but that night we made up for it.

In the morning, I called the office and told them I would be very late. I figured the market could do without me that morning. I had a life again. As June and I left the house to get some breakfast someplace, other than the café she works at, I reminded June, "Remember, you're going to come up with a name for this place."

"I'm working on it already, sweetheart," June assured me.

CHAPTER 7

WATCHING STOCKS

Fortunately, the market at that time was easy. Almost everything I bought for my clients went up. One of our clients, who trades a lot, comes into the office almost daily wanting to put more of his money to work. He claimed to be "long term," but he was really a stock trader at heart and usually had pretty good instincts. This particular client, I'll call JR. He is a lawyer whose firm is housed in our building. He is in our office almost daily checking his stocks and the overall market.

In fact, I'm sure that he checks his stocks and the market from the moment he gets up in the morning on his cell phone till he stops at our office on the way to his. JR has a large portfolio, mostly of stocks, and he is looking to enhance it any way he can.

Today, when he came in, I was trying to start the day off with a little humor. "JR, I'm glad that you stopped in today, because the phone in my limousine is busted, and I need some commission dollars to get it fixed."

JR answered right back, "Jay, do you expect me to feel sorry for you and fall for that old Eddie Murphy line and give you some easy business?" And then he went on to say, "What I need from you is some really good stock ideas that will make me some money right now."

"Well, JR," I shot right back, "I'm laying for you today, here's a list of fifteen 'Right Now' high-dividend paying stocks that our company recommends you buy immediately."

"Let me see that, Jay," he said as he grabbed my list. JR is quick; he buys two of them he likes, and wastes no time getting out the door to head upstairs to his office. I know he will be back before lunch to see how I did on the price buying the stocks. I like JR a lot, and so does everyone else in the office. I really have to be on my toes with JR. He is very sharp, well-read, and he has traveled all over the world and knows his current events worldwide as well. I was up to the task today, but I'm not sure what I will do tomorrow, especially if one of these stocks goes down. I know he will be watching.

After JR left, I told one of my team members, "I bet you that JR checks his stocks at least ten times a day. I think that someday I'm going to write a book and title it 'Closely watched stocks in Topeka, Kansas,'"

My mind, however, is not on the Dow Jones Averages or JR. I'm hoping that I'll maybe get a call yet today from June. A few moments later, my day dream comes true.

"Jay," the receptionist calls out, "pick up line two."

"Jay," June said, "my dad has had another one of his strokes and will be in the hospital for a while. Can you pick me up in the mornings every day, at least till he gets better?"

"Absolutely," I responded. "I'll see you tomorrow at 7:15."

June went on to say, "I don't have much time to talk because my mother is coming over to my apartment soon to pick me up to go to the hospital."

While I was sorry to hear that June's dad was in the hospital, I was very glad to get the chance every day to see and talk to June for the ten-minute ride from her apartment to the restaurant.

CHAPTER 8

KITTY MANSION

For several weeks now, June and I had been getting together as much as possible for dinner or once a week for all night at my home. I would also see her every morning, six days a week, to pick her up for work at the restaurant. When June was my waitress, she always came over to my table and we talked. She is very artistic, and sometimes she would show me cartoons she would draw the night before. These cartoons pictured me and my cats playing together. There was really a lot of humor in these cartoons, and they were of high-enough quality to have been in the Sunday newspaper.

"Jay," June said, "do you remember, a few weeks ago, I said we should have a name for this place?"

"I do, June, but I didn't come up with anything," I responded.

"Jay, I think we should call this place 'Kitty Mansion.'"

"June, I really like it, and I really think it fits." I went on to say, "Sweetheart, do you realize that with just two words, you have perfectly described this place?" June immediately began drawing a picture of a sign we could put on our mailbox for everyone to see. When she finished,

I rushed her drawing to a professional sign-maker's shop for them to make the sign that would fit on our mailbox. This sign would be bright red and big enough for everyone who passes to see. When I got the sign back, I put it proudly on the mailbox, so the next time June came over she could see it.

After that, whenever June and I came into the driveway, we looked at each other and smiled. I am sure that no one but June would ever have thought to name this stately old place Kitty Mansion. I hoped that at some time, in the future, June would be at Kitty Mansion permanently. She belonged there.

CHAPTER 9

RED AND GREEN SPOTLIGHTS

The old saying I mentioned before, "There's no fool like an old fool," didn't seem to apply to our relationship. The reason being June seemed more eager and happy with it than me. Initially, I said to myself, "I'm just going to go along with this while it lasts." I remember pinching myself to make sure I wasn't dreaming. That feeling soon gave way to the thought that I should take what we had as far as it could go. Why not? June seemed eager to do that same thing too. Neither one of us could wait to see each other every day when I picked her up.

In fact, one day on the way to work, June said, "Jay, why don't we kiss every time we pull up to a Stop sign or a red light and hold that kiss till the light changes to green?"

"Sweetheart, that sounds great to me," I quickly responded.

After that, whenever we stopped at a stoplight that was red, we kissed. I know this sounds a little silly, but I also know it was a lot more fun driving to work than I ever had in my life.

One morning, just after I picked up June, she asked, "Jay, do you just happen to have any paper I can write on?"

"June, I've got this old notebook in the back seat you can use," I responded as I reached back, got it, and handed it to her.

For the next ten minutes, we dispensed with the kissing while June wrote something rapidly in the notebook. I was real curious about what she was writing. When we got to the restaurant, as June was getting out of the car, she leaned back in and said, "Jay, hurry back to the restaurant after you park the car, and I will show this to you."

"Can't you show me now?" I asked.

"No, I'm almost late. Just get back as soon as you can," she repeated.

I sped over to where I could park and jogged back to the restaurant. Knowing that I wanted to see what it was that June wrote, June traded with another waitress and came quickly over to my table.

"Read this," she said. I did, and here's how it went:

PARADOX LOVE

When Green means Stop
And Red means go
That just proves
I Love you So

When Cracker Jacks
And wedding Vows
Fit together
I wonder how

Adopting Cats
Instead of Kids
That's what some Folks did

When 68
Meets 25
And the Girl won't even drive
Yet the feelings
Still Survive

You can Trust me
Yes or No
All this Proves
I LOVE YOU SO!

By June Hazel Burns

This short poem stopped me dead in my tracks for a few moments, and I was speechless. This short poem literally summed up things between us, and she wrote it in only ten minutes.

"Sweetheart," I said, "this is really wonderful."

"Oh, it's just a cheesy little thing," June said.

"You know I hate to admit it, but I couldn't write this in a week, and you did it in ten minutes," I responded.

Then it hit me. June wasn't just another pretty girl; she was a very brilliant and insightful pretty girl, and likely out of my league.

"June," I said, "can I take this to the office and make copies? I'll get it back to you when I see you tonight?"

"Go ahead," she responded. I made at least ten copies.

While June passed this off as just a silly little poem, I immediately loved it, but I couldn't help thinking that the forty-plus years difference in our age was not where we might have a problem. In short, she was way smarter than me, and I was going to have to brighten up a lot to keep up with her.

CHAPTER 10

OFFICER WARD (FICTIONAL)

One morning, when we were driving to work, we entered an area that is just in front of a new one-block-long law enforcement center just before we got to June's restaurant. This street had three potential stoplights to enjoy. But not today. It must have been a shift change, because just as soon as I stopped at the first red stoplight and we began kissing, here came a police car with lights flashing for me to pull over. I did pull over.

An officer came to my car and said, "You need to get out of your vehicle and give me your license and registration."

"Yes sir," I said. As he was looking at my license, I noticed that his nametag read *Officer Ward*.

Officer Ward then said, "According to this license, Mr. Sherrer, you are sixty-eight years old, is that correct?"

"Yes officer, that's correct."

Then officer Ward said, "You look a lot older in person than your picture."

Not something I was expecting or anxious to hear. "Officer Ward, I really appreciate you saying that, especially since it is a relatively new driver's license picture," I responded.

"You are probability wondering why I stopped you, Mr. Sherrer," Officer Ward said.

"Yes, I am," I said. "Well, when you and your lady friend were kissing at the stoplight, you were stopped too long after the light changed and were potentially holding up traffic," Officer Ward responded.

"But Officer Ward, there was no traffic behind me to hold up," I said.

"Doesn't matter," Officer Ward shot back, "you were still in a traffic lane and could have been blocking traffic too. Mr. Sherrer, I'm going to give you a break today, I'm only going to charge you with one count of inattentive driving, and not a second count of blocking a right-of-way," Officer Ward stated.

"Well, Officer Ward, I guess that should make me happy, but somehow I don't feel that way, and just what will that cost me?"

"One Hundred and fifty dollars plus court costs," Officer Ward answered. "Also, you must respond to this ticket within ten days or a warrant will be issued for your arrest," he added. "Mr. Sherrer, here's your paperwork, so get back into your car and proceed with caution," Officer Ward instructed.

As I was getting back in the car, June said, "I heard most of that and I can't believe it, especially the part about you looking older than the picture on you license."

"Believe me, that part really got me too," I added. "In fact, if I can't get things going tonight, you'll know why."

"Maybe I can help you do something about that," June added.

"Heck, it's only a hundred and fifty bucks anyway, and maybe my insurance company will overlook it," I said. "Let's just go on, and I'll try not to let it ruin our day," I concluded.

We started out again with Officer Ward following right behind. We came to the second stoplight in front of the law enforcement center in the middle of the block, and it was a red light too. This is when a smart man would not have done anything. But Jay Sherrer has not often been accused of being a smart man. I instinctively leaned over and passionately kissed June again. This was an especially passionate kiss. This time, both Officer Ward's lights and siren came on. You might have thought the world was coming to an end.

Officer Ward came over to my car again and said, "Young man, get out of your car and lean forward and put your hands on the hood."

"Well, at least it's young man this time," I said. This time he frisked me. He must have thought I was on something.

Office Ward then said, "I can't believe that you did the same thing again. This time I'm going to cite you again for inattentive driving and also blocking a right-of-way."

"Blocking a right of way!" I said exasperatedly. "You were the only one behind me. Were you in a big hurry to get to the doughnut shop?" I responded.

"I'm not going to answer that, Mr. Sherrer. Just stand there and wait a moment while I finish writing these two citations," Officer Ward instructed.

"I'm curious, Officer Ward, since you know how old I am, how old are you?" I asked.

"That's none of your business," Officer Ward shot back.

"Okay then, how long have you been on the force?" I asked.

"Seventeen years," Officer Ward answered proudly.

"It looks like you have only two stripes on your sleeve, and you're still writing traffic tickets," I added.

"Mr. Sherrer, you need to watch what you are saying, or I'll find something else to cite you with," Office Ward cautioned.

"Here are two more citations, Mr. Sherrer. You need to respond to these within ten days like the other ticket, Mr. Sherrer. Do you understand?"

"Yes," I responded. "Do you have anything else to say for yourself, Mr. Sherrer?"

"Well, Officer Ward, when you go home tonight and tell your wife you single-handedly cleaned up crime in Topeka today, I suggest that you leave out the part about giving three tickets to some old guy kissing his young girl-friend at a stoplight. Your wife might not think you have any romance left in your soul."

"I think I'm finished with you for now, Mr. Sherrer. Here are the last two of your three tickets." Officer Ward handed me the last two tickets. "Officer Ward, I do have a use for these three tickets. I have three bathrooms in my home, and these three tickets will come in handy. I'll have paper for each bathroom," I declared.

"Mr. Sherrer, you just need to get back in your car and proceed with caution and by the way, have a nice day," Officer Ward said, walling away.

When I limped back to the car, June said, "Sweetheart, I'm really sorry about this. I guess we should stop kissing at stoplights."

"*Never!*" I said. I paid the money, and yes, my insurance did raise my premiums, but I'm too much in love to care.

CHAPTER 11

THE KISS

Until June came along, my life was moving downhill. I had all but quit thinking that I could ever find someone who could take my mind off the market and everything else I thought was important. She did. June absolutely stopped me dead in my tracks and at last, I wasn't alone anymore.

One Friday morning, after delivering June to work, I parked the car and came back to the restaurant for a short breakfast. I had clients coming into my office in about forty-five minutes to work on a sizable estate, and I wasn't completely ready.

I said to June, "Sweetheart, I'm in a hurry this morning, so get me my breakfast as soon as possible."

She did, rang up my ticket, and I was out the door in a flash. I started walking down the street toward the building I worked in when I heard something behind me. I turned and saw it was June running toward me.

As she was about to get to me, she said, "You left so fast I didn't get a chance to say goodbye." At that point, she jumped into my arms and I dropped my briefcase, and we kissed passionately as we were turning around and around.

Cars passing by were honking their horns, so we just kissed more. When we did stop kissing, June and I walked backward as she was going back to the restaurant and me to my office building.

As she was about to the restaurant door, June shouted, *"I love you!"*

And I shouted it right back, "I love you more, sweetheart!"

Looking back on it, it seems like something two kids would do, but I didn't care. I knew it was finally true love for me, and my love for June was making an old guy like me look very foolish, but love has no age limits, and I didn't care what it looked like.

Then June waved once more and disappeared into the restaurant. I waved back to her, and I then turned back to resume my two-block walk to my office building. I next passed through a large parking lot where two four-month-old kittens had been staying. Their mother had left them when they were just three months old. I had been bringing them food and water twice a day, and I was planning on bringing them to Kitty Mansion soon. I was all they had. The minute they saw me coming, they came running to me from halfway across the parking lot. I had plenty of food and water for them in my briefcase, and I made sure I had the treats they liked too.

I then sprinted to my office to get there just before the market opening. After the market opened, I did a few orders left over from yesterday. I am now ready to focus on my meeting coming up. I hurriedly finished my proposal, and went to one of the copiers to make copies for everyone. When I started making copies, something very strange happened. I got a really very big hard-on at the copier. I was stunned. I hadn't had one like this for at least five years. It must have been a delayed reaction from the great kiss June gave me moments ago. The thought occurred to me since I was at the copier with my back to everyone. Why not take it out and copy it so I could show it off to June later tonight?

I looked both ways to see if anyone was watching to unzip my pants, and as I was just about to do it, the receptionist yelled, "Jay, you're wanted on line one!"

That killed it, because I had to run back to my desk and take care of that call. When the call was over, so was my hard-on. As the call was ending, I could also see my clients coming through the door to our office about fifteen minutes early. The hard-on was gone for now, but I told myself I could still get it up. I hoped it would happen again soon and I couldn't wait to tell June.

Later in the day, when I was going home, I always stopped on my way to my car again with more food and water for the same two kittens. A few weeks later, I was able to bring them to Kitty Mansion. I hoped the other cats would accept them. They needed a real home.

CHAPTER 12

FIRST HOSPITAL STAY

It was late Wednesday night, about 11 p.m., and I was home napping when my phone rang. Thinking that it might be June calling to say good night, I grabbed the phone without looking at the caller ID first. Instead, to my surprise, it was June's mother, Leslie. Leslie is a straightforward, very direct Christian woman. Up to this point, on the few times I have met or spoken with her, she was friendly to me, even though probably, at my age, I doubt if I would have been someone she would have picked for her daughter. I was at least eight years older than Leslie and over forty years older than June.

Leslie got right to the point. "June and I are in the emergency room at Stormont Vail Hospital, because June had apparently been drinking a lot at her apartment, and she started vomiting and couldn't quit. She called me, and I rushed over to her apartment and brought her here." She went on to say, "Jay, I hate to tell you this, but for the last six years, June has been addicted to alcohol, and we had to take her out of college and put her in rehab five years ago." Leslie finished by adding, "I have to leave here soon because

I have to go to work early tomorrow. Can you come to the hospital now and stay with her 'til they decide if they are going to admit her?"

"Sure I can, Leslie," I said while I was trying to wake up quickly. "I'll be there in fifteen minutes," I promised. Stormont Vail Hospital was in the middle of town, about six miles from Kitty Mansion.

Hurriedly, I threw on some clothes and a jacket and drove right to the hospital. June's mother came out to the emergency room waiting room where I was stopped to give them permission for me to be allowed into the cubicle June was in. Leslie said that one of the hospital doctors was just in and they were going to take her to get x-rays soon.

Leslie gave me her phone number and said, "Jay, call me when they decide what they are going to do with her."

I told Leslie, "I will stay with June if it takes all night, and I'll let you know what they decide." Before Leslie left, being very religious, she grabbed both our hands and led us in prayer for June. I got the feeling that June's mother had been praying a lot for her.

So far, June had been on IVs for the past two hours and given medicine to help her stop vomiting for now. After June's mother left, June and I looked at each other. I could see a tear streaming down her cheek. She spoke first in a shaky voice, "Jay, I guess you now know why I left college my senior year and have never finished since then.

"Sweetheart," I said softly, "you don't have to explain. We'll figure college out later. I'm not ever leaving your side, not now or forever!" I was holding June's hand when a nurse came in to wheel her to get x-rays. Even though June was gone only fifteen minutes, it seemed like forever.

Shortly after June was brought back to the room, a doctor came in. She said that they would be keeping June for a while and they were readying a room for her, but first they needed more blood work, and another nurse came in for the blood work.

The doctor looked June directly in the face and said, "June, you have just had an acute, alcohol-induced, pancreatitis attack. You have to *stop drinking!* If you don't *stop drinking,* you will *die soon!* Do you understand?" June nodded her head that she did.

At that point, I slipped out of the room to call Leslie to let her know what the doctor said and that June would be staying the night and probably several other nights as well. It was well after one o'clock in the morning before we were headed to a room for now, until a room in the ICU opened up.

When we got to the room, June was given something to help her sleep. While she was still awake, I said, "Honey, I'll call your job and let them know where you are and that you might not be in for maybe a week."

"Okay," June faintly responded before she fell asleep. It was about 2:30 in the morning before I lifted my hand from June's hand and kissed her gently on her forehead so as not to wake her, and left the hospital. Visiting hours started at 7:30 in the morning, and I intended to be at June's side the very next morning at that time when she woke up.

CHAPTER 13

AUNT TILDA

True to my word, I was back to the hospital early the next morning, waiting for visiting hours to begin at 7:30 a.m. After the morning nursing crew took over, June was a little shaky, but she was able to smile that beautiful smile she has when I came into her room.

"June," I said, trying to look disappointed, "you sure picked a tough way to get out of our Thursday night date."

"Well, Jay, I guess you can spend it here with me in my room," June responded faintly. She went on to say, "it would be great if you could sneak in a hamburger and fries for me. They have me eating ice chips, and I'm starting to get hungry."

"You know, sweetheart, all these machines you are hooked up to would go off like you hit a jackpot at a casino when you took your first bite, and at least three nurses would rush in here knowing something was really wrong. When they found out what it was, they would throw me out," I pleaded.

"I guess you're right," June sighed. I pulled a chair up close to June's bed so I could hold her hand. She was definitely better than last night, but still very shaky

After a few minutes passed, a hospital doctor came in and asked June several questions about how she was feeling, and he felt her stomach to see if she had any pain in certain areas. While she had no real pain in her kidney and liver areas, she was having a lot of discomfort in her pancreas area.

The doctor said, "June, I'm going to prescribe something for your pain."

"Thank you, Doctor," June responded. He went on to say, "So far, we are finding no real kidney or liver damage."

This doctor, we would find out, was really good, had a lot of empathy and care for his patients, and he visited June often in the mornings. He tried to cheer June up with a little humor too but still firmly warned her about her drinking. We both really appreciated his visits. Both he and I were hoping this would be a wake-up call for June to quit her drinking. If we were rating doctors, both June and I agreed he was five-star.

I had started sort of a schedule. I was coming to the hospital early in the morning at exactly 7:30 a.m. and staying until 8:30 a.m., then leaving for my office. I usually had June to myself at that time in the morning. Then I would drop by in the afternoons briefly after the market closed. Then I'd go home to feed my kittens and come back from around 7:30 p.m. till 9 p.m. when visiting hours were over. This would give other family and friends time to see her through the day. June's pastor and several church members often visited her during the day. June and her mother,

Leslie, were long-time church members, and several of them came to see her every day. They were very concerned about June and had known about her drinking problem for some time.

However, on the third day, at around 3:30, in the afternoon, I stopped on the way to June's room and bought some flowers for her—even though I knew June preferred dandelions. It was Christmastime, and we had snow on the ground, and there were no dandelions to be found. She even likes dandelions so much she has one tattooed on her ankle. When I got to her room, a rather large woman was standing resolutely in the doorway, blocking me from entering the room.

She said quite loudly, "June doesn't want to see you, not now or anymore. I'm her aunt, and she doesn't want you coming here anymore!"

"That can't be right!" I shot back.

"You're a PEDOPHILE!" she yelled loudly so at least everyone on that floor could hear it. "PEDOPHILE, PEDO-PHILE, PEDOPHILE!" she kept yelling. I know she was prob-ably hoping I would hit her so she could charge me with something. Instead, I tried once again to calmly ask her to move so I could enter June's room.

She continued to yell, "You're a PEDOPHILE!" I decided to go down the hall about twenty yards to a nurses' station to try to get some help with the situation. I turned back as I got to the station, and I could see that she was headed for the elevator. At about the same time, June had worked her way out of all the drips and monitors she had hooked to her to come out of her room, to rescue me, and bring me back.

"Are you okay?" she asked.

"Yeah, I guess, but I think your aunt got a large hunk out of my already scrawny ass before she left."

"Jay, why don't we both hold on to each other so we can get back to the room?" June asked.

"Sure," I replied.

When we got back to the room and the nurses came in to reconnect June to all the stuff she had been connected to, I said, "Here are some slightly wilted flowers that have been through a lot just getting to you. I know you would prefer candy, but I don't think they want you to eat any candy just yet."

"Jay, they're really lovely anyway, and I am flattered that you got them for me," June assured me.

"Jay, I don't think they plan for me to leave here soon, because they are still wanting to move me to ICU when a room opens up," June mentioned.

"June," I asked, "didn't your grandmother send you and your mom tickets to fly back to Atlanta to see her over Christmas?"

"Yes, she did," June replied. "Until they can get me into ICU, they are having someone come in at night and sit with me, so that when I go into withdrawal, I won't do something to hurt myself. Christmas is next week, Jay, and I'm not sure I will be out of the hospital and able to go. Look at this bracelet they put on my wrist, it says FALL RISK." June held her arm out to show me. The nurses had given June something to relax her after this afternoon's events. So when she fell asleep, I kissed her forehead and left for the day, knowing that her mother and some church friends were coming to be with June later that night.

When I came in the next morning early to see June, she smiled a little for me and handed me something she wrote late last night after my encounter with her aunt.

LOVE ON DECEMBER 22 {For JAY}

That "Sticks and Stones" bit isn't true,
'Cause words can cut you through &
through

But if that's the game you want to play,
Just save your breath is what I say.

Pity, people do not see
The love, like that of you and me

It's all around unrecognized,
But people choose to close their eyes.

So let them talk & let them stare,
It's sad they'll never see what's there.

For we have armor you can't see
Protecting us from enemies.

The more you fire your flaming tongue
The stronger grows our will as one.

Save petty, spite & hatred too,
In fact, it's only hurting you.

But go & try now, if you must,
The weaker you, the stronger us.

If not by word or action too,
With honesty I'll prove to you:
I love you, Jay, with all my heart.

Written by June Hazel Burns

When I read this poem, it brought tears to my eyes. I knew she was still in physical distress and heavily medicated, and she was able to write this to help me.

CHAPTER 14

FIRST HOSPITAL STAY
CONTINUED

When I returned to the hospital the evening of the fourth day, June was sitting in a padded chair. Maybe I should say, literally strapped into the chair with a nurse sitting close by. She tried to speak, but the words were twisted around to where it was very difficult for me to understand her. The nurse called me aside and said, "June is going through withdrawal, and we have to restrain her and watch her closely to see that she does not harm herself." She went on to say, "We hope to move her very soon to ICU so that we can monitor her closer." I stayed with her for a little longer until they gave her something to help her sleep. After June fell asleep, the nurse assured me they would be watching her closely, so I left for the day.

The next morning, I got a call from Leslie (June's mother). "Jay, June has been moved to ICU, and I will make arrangements for you to be allowed to see her, since you are not family."

"I really appreciate that, Leslie," I replied. When June was out of her withdrawal, a psychiatrist was brought in to help June deal with her emotional problems. Even though June's medical scores were improving, it was now for sure June would not be out of the hospital in time for her to go with her mother to Atlanta to be with her grandparents for Christmas. So that I could be with June in the hospital over Christmas, I called my sister, who lives a few hundred miles away and told her I would not be making it home for Christmas at her ranch this year.

After June was much better, she was scheduled to be released in a few days, a pair of social workers came to visit her. Both of these ladies had, in years gone past, the same drinking problems June was having. One of them told June, "I can tell you for sure that if you keep drinking, it will eventually kill you, June." She went on to say, "You have to stop now!"

The second one handed June a piece of paper listing the different rehabilitation centers that could help her with her drinking problem in our area that June should consider going to.

June and I looked at the list and she said, "I've been to two of these centers already and they were terrible." I grabbed the list anyway because I didn't think June would keep it.

June was now back on regular food, and some physical therapists were coming in two to three times a day to help her with her walking. She had told me, "Jay, I think that they are going to release me tomorrow."

"Sweetheart, if you call me when they are about to release you, I'll come right over and get you and take you to your apartment."

That would make it the fourth day after Christmas, and June had missed her trip to Atlanta to see her family. I was planning on picking her up, so I got to work early to get a few things done, then call her, but I got a call from June to tell me, "Jay, my dad has already brought me from the hospital to my apartment, but I can go out to dinner with you tonight, if you want?"

"Sure thing, I'll pick you up at six," I responded.

After dinner, I got June right back to her apartment. I held her in my arms and gave her a long good-night kiss. "Sweetheart," I said, "is there anything I can do to help you quit drinking?"

"Jay, just try to hang in there with me, but I know I need to do most of it myself," June responded.

"June, I love you and I'll always be there for you," I promised.

CHAPTER 15

VISIT FROM GRANDMOTHER

Moving forward about a month, after leaving the hospital, when June wasn't working she was staying with her mother two nights a week and spending the rest of her time at her apartment or with me at Kitty Mansion. On one of the mornings I was picking her up at her apartment to go to work, June seemed somewhat excited.

When we pulled out of the drive to her apartment, she said, "Guess what, Jay?"

"What?" I answered.

"My grandmother and aunt on my mother's side of the family are coming to town from Atlanta on Tuesday, and we are all going out to dinner. And here's the best part—you are invited to go to dinner with us too!" June said excitedly.

"Well, that's nice, but do you really want me there, considering that things didn't go so well the last time I met one of your family?" I responded.

"What kind of remark is that, Jay?" June argued. "Sure, I do, I want to show you off," June proclaimed.

"Okay, Tuesday it is. Let me know when you want me to pick you up," I responded.

"I will," June replied.

I know, from everything June has said to me, that she is very close to her grandmother and aunt from Atlanta, and they would definitely have heard from June about me by now. But I knew I still needed to be on my best behavior.

Tuesday came around fast, and I was worried. Right now, as it stands, I'm batting five hundred. June's mom seems to be "okay" with me, but her dad and her aunt on her dad's side of the family are definitely not thrilled with me. I'm hoping that will change.

For dinner they all wanted to go to Olive Garden, so June told them we would meet them there. When I meet people who are new to me, I try to let them talk first and not dominate the conversation. Within a few moments, I could see that this side of the family was delightful. June's family knew June's good points and her weakness, especially for alcohol, so no one ordered any liquor. The conversation was good, and I deferred to June whenever I could. June has numerous talents, including drawing cartoons of my cats, and I brought several of them to show off, but I never got a chance. Besides, I think they already knew about that talent.

June's aunt asked me, "Jay, what do you think about the market right now?"

"Recently I told one of my fellow brokers that the way the market is moving up, almost anything I do for my clients goes up," I replied.

June and I were definitely in great, friendly company. My worries were misplaced. They seemed to be unconcerned about our age difference. They just wanted June to be happy. I grabbed the check as fast as I could, but I don't think that mattered to them.

About a week later, June handed me an unopened letter sent to her from her grandmother.

June said, "My grandmother sent this to me to give to you."

"Really?" I responded as I was opening the letter. I almost immediately closed the card and put it back in the letter.

June said, "You didn't even read the card."

"Yes, I did. What you don't know is that I'm a speed reader," I proclaimed.

"Well, Mr. Speed Reader, tell me what it said," June insisted.

"Okay," I said while holding on tightly to the letter. She thanked me for paying for our dinner, and she said she hoped to come back soon, and hoped she and I could go out for dinner again. "There was a PS on the letter too," I added.

"What was that?" June demanded.

"She said, no need to bring June along this time," I said, trying to keep from laughing.

"What?" June yelled as she grabbed the letter out my hands. "It doesn't say that, you jerk."

"Well, I really had you going for a while," I said with a big smile.

June smiled back and said, "You know this is going to hurt your chances later tonight" My big smile faded quickly.

CHAPTER 16

THERAPIST

Shortly after June's mother returned from her Christmas visit to her mother and dad's home in Atlanta, she advised June, "June, I think that since you're not going to rehab, you should be going to a good 'Christian' therapist."

"Mom, I can agree to that, but I don't know who that might be," June responded.

"I'll ask around with some of my church friends and see if I can come up with someone," Leslie replied.

"Okay," June agreed.

A few weeks later, Leslie told us, "A therapist named Shane Williams keeps coming up with some of my friends. You might contact him."

June did contact Shane and arranged to start treatment with him on a twice-a-week basis late in the afternoons after I got off work. Looking back on things, even though it didn't stop June from drinking, the time June spent with Shane, one on one, proved to be one of the best things she could have done over a six-year period to help her deal with several of her emotional problems. In fact, I could see a big improvement in June's spirit after her hour-long sessions with Shane.

After only a few sessions with Shane, June said to me as we were driving home, "Shane is really easy to talk to, and he has some great suggestions on how I might approach things. In fact, you might want to start going to him too, Jay."

"I'll sure consider that, but I think for now we can only afford for one of us to go, sweetheart."

"Hey," June responded, "I forgot to tell you that my mom called today and said that my grandmother is sending me a thousand dollars to help with the cost of my sessions with Shane."

"That's really great, honey," I replied.

CHAPTER 17

MOVING TO KITTY MANSION

The apartment June lived in was ideal for her. The owners had remodeled the basement for their daughter and son-in-law to live in. They, however, moved out, so the owners, who were good church friends with June's mother, decided to rent it to June. It was spacious, with a private entrance, and no utility bills. June loved it. She also liked the independence it gave to her.

At about 2 a.m. one morning, a few months after she got out of the hospital, I got a frantic phone call from June. She was struggling to speak without crying.

"Jay," she said, "I have to move out in two months. I'm on the bench outside my apartment smoking, and earlier this evening the landlord posted a note on my door saying that their daughter needed to move back into the apartment. Jay, I have to be out in two months," she repeated.

"Sweetheart, I know how much you love that place, but, what the heck? I've got plenty of room here if you don't mind all of the kitties. Why not come live with me?"

"Really? I could move in with you?" June asked.

"Absolutely, you are here a lot anyway," I added. "And I know you can really cook as well, so I think it could work out," I explained.

"Really?" June repeated, "I could move to Kitty Mansion?"

"Certainly!" I assured her. "Maybe, knowing I have a place to go to, I can get some sleep, Jay," June finished.

"Sweetheart, get some sleep because I'll be there at 7:15 tomorrow morning to pick you up. We can talk about it more then," I added.

After hanging up the phone, I got up to take a few more sleeping pills—something I needed to taper way down on with myself. I realized I hadn't lived with a woman since my ex-wife moved out over twenty-five years ago. I was apprehensive about it, but I knew that having June live with me would help me monitor June's drinking. It also might help me get younger and not die this irrelevant, senile old man I was rapidly becoming before I met June.

Even though we had sixty days for June to move out of her apartment and into Kitty Mansion, June was making headway already. When I arrived to pick her up the very next morning, June was waiting on the bench in front of her apartment with a few boxes of nonessential things.

June said, "Jay, unlock your trunk so I can put these boxes in, and I can start with the move a little bit at a time."

"Sounds like a good plan to me, sweetheart," I responded. "I'll put all your boxes in my empty family room downstairs until we get time to sort through everything," I added.

On our way to the restaurant, I told June, "Up 'til now, I've only been living in a few rooms of my house, the master bedroom and bath, the kitchen, and I occasionally make a fire in the fireplace. About three years ago, when I didn't have many kitties, I had a large garage sale, and if someone showed any interest in anything, I just gave it to them. I needed to get rid of stuff I've built up over the years. I was halfway considering buying a condominium downtown, close to the office where I work. Now I'm really glad I didn't do that move. Since you're moving in, having this place makes sense to me again."

"Jay, I know I can get rid of some of my stuff, and if you do the same, I know we can make it work," June assured me. "June, we are starting a new adventure together," I added with a kiss.

CHAPTER 18

COUNTDOWN TO FINAL MOVING DAY

The two-month notice went by quickly, and my downstairs room and garage were filling up. One of my coworkers at my office had a big F-150 Ford truck and helped us move June's heavier pieces the Saturday morning before the last weekend. We were very grateful. At that point, June was actually living with me full-time.

June's last official day in her apartment was going to be our cleaning day. She was going to clean really hard to try to get her $250.00 deposit back. June told me the Friday before, "Jay, I'm going to take Saturday off, and my mom and I are going to really clean up the apartment so that maybe I can get my deposit back. Can you help us?"

"Sweetheart, I wouldn't miss it for the world. Besides, I've got this new, really good carpet cleaner that needs a good workout. I'll do the best I can," I promised.

June's mom, Leslie, cleans houses for a living, so she took charge. "June, you take the icebox, and Jay, you start with your carpet cleaner in the living room for now," she directed.

After I finished the living room carpet, Leslie directed me to June's bedroom. When I got to the large, walk-in closet, I was somewhat shocked to find three large bottles of vodka buried in the back. I waited till I was sure no one was watching, and I took them outside, poured them out in the driveway, and hid the empties inside a large trash can. I began to realize that helping June through her drinking problem was going to be harder than I thought. June was definitely a very serious drinker. It was good that she would be living with me because I would be better able to help reduce the liquor coming into Kitty Mansion. Or at least I thought I could. June had been drinking a lot of hard liquor daily, and her body was now giving out.

Later that day, June's landlord came by, inspected the almost—spotlessly—clean apartment, and gave June back her deposit.

I told June, "Well, sweetheart, thanks to the awesome help from your mom, we were able to get your deposit back."

June said, "Jay, I should probably give this deposit to you since I'm coming to live with you."

"Hey, gal, why don't you save that in some kind of fund to help you go back to college sometime soon?" I replied.

June gave me a long, puzzled, and bewildered look, then said, "I doubt I will be doing that anytime soon." I let it drop, but I knew that at some point in time, for her to advance beyond being a waitress, she needed to go back to college and finish up. Obviously, June wasn't ready to do that at this time.

After a long day cleaning and moving the last of June's stuff out of the apartment to my car, I told June,

"Sweetheart, when we get to the house, I'll go get us a pizza while you put the stuff from your refrigerator to mine. Okay?

"Sounds good to me," June responded.

After I got back with the pizza, I built a big fire in the fireplace at Kitty Mansion, and we relaxed in front of it and ate our pizza. We both tried to forget, for now, that we had a major job ahead of us putting stuff away and finding out if we could live together in harmony.

CHAPTER 19

DRINKING AGAIN AND
THEN REPEAT

Even with expert counseling, in a matter of a few weeks, I was fairly certain June was drinking again. One or two large bottles of vodka a day. She was very good at hiding the bottles from me. When she went to her mother's house for the evening, I would search her bedroom and bathroom for bottles, and I often found one or two. I poured them out and hoped that would be the last of them. I had listened to the doctors during June's last hospital stay. They repeatedly told June that she would die if she didn't quit drinking. The very thought of that was almost more than I could handle. I kept telling myself, "Jay, you've got to be strong, you've got to be strong." My longtime partner and close friend at work was dying of lymphoma. I could see him failing more every day when he could make it to work. And June was drinking herself to death at the same time. When I could, I tried to take off from work early and pick June up as she got off work at 2:30 so she wouldn't get a ride from a friend who might include a stop at a liquor store. June often carried a large handbag. I was naive enough not to suspect she had a smaller bottle of vodka with her, but she often did.

On the way to work one morning, I noticed June was not saying much. I asked her, "Sweetheart, is there something wrong?"

"Jay," she responded, "I think I might be fired today."

"Why do you think that?"

"Yesterday the manager caught me drinking on the job again, and she said she was going to talk to the owner," June said, almost crying. "I just can't help it, Jay. It seems like I have to drink to cope with my feelings."

"Honey, is there anything I can do to help you more than I have been?" I asked.

"No, Jay, you've been doing a lot for me as it is," June said.

When we got to the restaurant, I waited, and, sure enough, June was let go. June left the restaurant crying, so I took her back to Kitty Mansion and stayed with her till she was better and could get some sleep. Then I went to the office. Even though the waitress job was way below June's abilities, it was the only full-time job she had since she had to leave college a few years ago due to her drinking. There was not much of a chance she could get another to replace it any time soon. June also felt bad because a lot of people enjoyed coming into the restaurant to visit with her. I'm sure business really fell off for them when June wasn't there anymore.

Even though there were lots of things to do around the house while putting away stuff, this was a really low point for her. I was trying to think of things we could do to take her mind off things. I got to thinking that Topeka has a really great zoo, and this would be a great time for us to go.

"June, what about I take off early tomorrow, and we go to the zoo?" I asked.

June responded, after wiping her tears from her eyes, somewhat uplifted, "Okay, Jay, that sounds like it could be fun."

The zoo was a great idea, and June's mom, Leslie, even came along too. June was able to relax and enjoy a few hours away from her troubles.

It just so happened that a week later, June's church and other churches in Kansas were having a three-day women's retreat at a camp near Wichita, Kansas. June's mother convinced June to go. It would be three days of Christian fellowship with people June had known and liked for years, and hopefully no drinking.

June said to me, "Jay, if I'm going to go, I need a new sleeping bag. I don't think the old one I had when I was a kid will do."

"Sweetheart, I can handle that," I responded. In less than three hours, I had the best sleeping bag Walmart had and bought a lot of extra minutes for June's cell phone so she could call me often. I was hoping this retreat would be good for June since she would constantly be around her mother and a lot of other gals she grew up with, and would not have many chances to drink.

The night before she was to leave, June came to me and said, "Jay, even though this trip with my mom and several of my old girl friends should be good for me, I'm still going to miss you and all the kitties a lot."

"Sweetheart, that's nice for me to hear, but I know you could definitely stand to take a break from all of this stuff you have been sorting through, and you've cooked up a lot of my favorite food for me to eat while you are gone. Remember, you have plenty of minutes on your cell phone so you can call me often," I responded.

"I'll be sure to call you a lot," June promised.

Later that Thursday afternoon, I got the call I wanted to hear from June.

"Honey, we're here!" June said excitedly.

"That's great," I responded. "They tell us we are all getting candles and we are going on a candlelight walk to a service after dark. It sounds exciting," June added.

"Sounds like fun," I said.

"I've got to go now, but I'll call you later if I can. Love you," June finished.

Later that evening, I got a call again from June.

June closed with, "Jay, we're back to the lodge now and ready to turn in. They are getting us up early for breakfast and classes tomorrow morning, so I need to try to get some sleep. Got to go now. Love you."

I quickly closed with, "Love you back." Unfortunately, this was one of the last calls I got from June for the next two days. I hesitated to call June because, after all, this was supposed to be a short getaway for her and a time for her to hopefully get refocused on her life and not to be drinking.

That hope was shattered when I got a frantic call from June's mom late Sunday afternoon.

"Jay, shortly after we got back to the church, June blacked out in the ladies' bathroom, and we had to call an ambulance to revive her and take her to the hospital. I don't know how she did it, but she must have been drinking a lot of the time we were at the retreat."

"Leslie, I'll get dressed and meet you at the emergency room as soon as I can," I responded. This was definitely not a good finish to what I had hoped would be a fun time for June and her mother.

CHAPTER 20

SECOND HOSPITAL STAY

When I got to the hospital emergency room, Leslie met me there. Leslie said, "June had hit her head when she blacked out in the church bathroom, and they just took her to get x-rays, but she should be back in maybe fifteen minutes."

"Jay, I skipped some of my cleaning jobs last week to go on the retreat, so I'm going to need to leave soon because I need to get up early to do some of that work first thing Monday morning," Leslie explained.

"Leslie, I'm ready to stay all night if needed," I replied. After June got back to the emergency room from her x-rays, I grabbed her hand to help her relax some. She had been through a lot over the past few hours. A hospital doctor came into the room and spoke to June about the x-rays, but he repeated the same warning as before: "IF YOU DON'T STOP DRINKING, YOU WILL DIE."

Leslie left shortly after we all joined hands and prayed. At about 11 p.m., they finally had a private room open up and they wheeled her there with me trailing behind with June's belongings. They had given June something to help her sleep, but it hadn't kicked in yet. After we got settled in the room and her nurses all talked to her and left, I could see June was getting ready to sleep.

June looked at me with tears in her eyes and said, "Jay, I guess the retreat didn't turn out so well."

"Honey," I responded, "you've had a really tough day, but maybe sometime you'll look back and remember some of the good times you all had. Anyhow," I added, "at least you got out of the house and away from me for a while."

June smiled a little as she brushed away her tears and said, "Jay, I missed you the whole time." June went on to say, "Jay, it's got to be past midnight, and you have the stock market opening up soon, so why don't you go home and get at least some sleep?"

"Sweetheart, I'm not at all worried about that, so I think I'll wait here until you go to sleep."

"You don't have to. The nurses will be in here checking on me every ten minutes," June pleaded.

"I'll stay a while anyway."

I stayed until about 1 a.m. as I softly sang the lyrics to our favorite song to her. "You are my sunshine, my only sunshine. You make me happy when skies are gray. You'll never know, dear, how much I love you. Please don't take my sunshine away."

I got home at about 1:30 a.m. and counted all my kitties' noses to make sure everyone was home and all right. I planned to sleep about three hours and go back to the hospital by 7:30 a.m. when visiting hours started and spend at least a half hour with June before going to the office.

When I got back to June's room early Monday morning, she was being helped from the bathroom back to her freshly changed bed. June was shaking and still sleepy from the sleeping medicine they had given her. She was surprised I made it back so quickly.

I spoke first to ask her, "How are you doing, sweetheart?"

"I'm feeling very weak and they still haven't come back with the results of my blood work," June replied. "How are all the kitties doing?" June asked.

"They are great, but the inside kitties that see you a lot are missing you already," I responded. "Has the hospital doctor been by to see you yet this morning?"

"Not yet, but he will probably be by soon," June replied. "Jay, I'm supposed to see Shane Wednesday for my therapy appointment. Could you call him and cancel the appointments for the rest of the week? I think I'll be here for a while?" June asked.

"I'll do that just as soon as I get to the office," I replied.

Just before I was about to leave, the hospital doctor came into June's room. He had the blood work results.

"June, you have had another alcohol-induced acute pancreatitis attack," the doctor said. "You have to quit drinking. You are fortunate that, so far, your liver and kidneys are not materially affected," he added. "You were in here six months ago with the same problem, and unfortunately your body is now weaker than before. Your recovery will probably be slower than last time. We will move you to a room in ICU when one becomes available. Do you have any questions?" he asked.

"No doctor," June answered.

"I will check back later this morning when you have had more time to rest," the doctor said as he left the room.

Just as he was leaving, another nurse came in to take more blood for more tests.

I told June, "Later today, I'm sure a lot of people, especially from the church, will be by to visit you, so I will wait 'til after dinner to come back."

"Okay, Jay," June replied faintly. I kissed her forehead and left for my office.

CHAPTER 21

SECOND HOSPITAL
STAY CONTINUED

Things were going along much like June's last visit six months ago, except June had lost most of her ability to walk unassisted. I was especially impressed with the hospital doctors who were treating June. Their message was really clear: "Stop drinking or it will only get worse for you." Luckily, at this point, they had not found noticeable kidney or liver damage.

Later that week, while I was visiting June, two ladies who had been approved by the hospital came by her room to visit June again. They had another list of rehabilitation facilities locally or that were within a hundred-mile radius of Topeka. Once June was out of the hospital, they urged her to visit these centers and talk to them about enrolling in one of their programs.

After they left, I said to June, "Why don't I check several of these out now and see what they have to offer?"

"Jay," June said, "I've already been to two of these on the list, so we can cross them off, but if you want to talk to these others, go ahead and we can at least consider something after I get out and can walk again."

"Sweetheart, that's a start anyway. I'll work on it," I promised. "I know we have to get treatment for you to help you get over this problem," I added. For the first time, June seemed to reluctantly agree.

June's hospital stay looked like it was going to be a few days longer than last time because she was having a lot of difficulty getting up and walking on her own. The hospital physical therapy people were working with her several times daily. After work, I was calling and visiting places locally that I thought might be able to help her on an out-patient basis. After a few days of afternoon visits, I found one that I liked and was anxious to tell June about later that evening.

June is a popular gal and a lot of her friends and family were stopping by to visit her through the day, so I usually tried to make my visits early before anyone else was there and later in the evening after most of the other visitors had left. June was now in the ICU, so visiting hours ended at nine. Late in the evening, just before visiting hours ended, I was able to talk to June alone to tell her what I found out about the alcohol center here locally that I thought might help her.

"Sweetheart," I said, "the one center I visited on the list those ladies gave us that I think we should visit has group classes three nights a week for three hours, plus they have therapists available that you can book individual meetings with. What do you think about that?" I asked.

"Jay, it sounds like it might be worth considering, but right now I'm still working with the physical therapy people at the hospital because I'm not really able to walk much on my own. They have me going to the Kansas Physical Rehabilitation Center just across the street from the hospital, every weekday for four hours for about a month after I get released from the hospital," June said with a discouraged look on her face.

"Honey, I'll be right by your side every day helping you do whatever it takes, and we also have Shane helping too," I assured her. We stopped talking for a few moments because visiting hours were about over. I held June's hand until the bell rang for visitors to leave, then I kissed her and left for the evening.

CHAPTER 22

REHABILITATION
(BODY AND HAIR)

When we were leaving the hospital, I made sure I had a good grip on June's shoulder because she was very unsteady on her feet. One of the hospital doctors had written her a prescription to go to the Kansas Rehabilitation Center for three days a week, up to four hours a day. This was for physical therapy so June could get her coordination back and be able to walk again without assistance. The prescription was for a one-month period. The center decided it would be best for her if she came in from 10 a.m. to 12 p.m. in the mornings and back again from 3 p.m. to 5 p.m. on Mondays, Wednesdays, and Fridays.

After a few weeks, on our way home from one of the afternoon sessions, June said to me, "Jay, I've been mostly working with one of the senior physical therapists, and she is really good. Her name is Karen, and she has taken a real interest in me."

"Honey, that doesn't surprise me because I've noticed from day one that you are genuinely interested in almost anyone you meet. That's a quality that makes people comfortable being around you," I responded.

"I really like being around her, not just with the therapy, but we talk a lot too," June added.

Because this had become an all-around good time for June, I didn't mind taking a break from the office to get June back and forth from her appointments. I knew during that time she definitely would not be drinking. I almost hated to see this month-long period come to an end. When it did, I was thankful to see that June was physically mostly recovered and seemed happy with her life again too.

One evening, after one of her afternoon sessions, June was taking a shower. After the shower, June came over to me with a clump of her hair in her hands.

"Jay, look at this!" June said frantically. "I'm losing my hair by the handful."

"I hadn't noticed 'til now, honey. Let me get some light on your head so I can look at it more closely," I said while getting a flashlight. After looking June's hair over carefully, I said, "Sweetheart, it sure does look like you've lost a lot of hair. Have you been taking your multivitamins daily?"

"Yes," June replied. "Maybe we can get some vitamins just for hair, and it will stop this hair loss. What do you think?" June asked.

"We sure can. In fact, I'll ask the pharmacist tomorrow what they recommend," I replied.

"Jay, I'll go with you tomorrow and help you look for something," June added. We found the hair vitamins and June started taking them every day, but her hair kept falling out at a rapid pace.

About two weeks later, June said to me, "Jay, I've gone online, and it seems like Bosley's Hair Care specializes in hair loss problems. They have a branch office in Kansas City on the Plaza just an hour away. Can we go soon?"

"Sure, go ahead and call them and book an appointment on a Saturday, if you can," I replied. I was eager to try to do something about June's hair loss problem so she would have less stress and maybe she wouldn't drink.

When I got home from work the very next day, June greeted me at the door, and she was very excited. "Guess what, Jay?" she blurted out. "I've got a 2 p.m. appointment at Bosley's for this coming Saturday afternoon at the Plaza office."

"That's a deal," I replied. "Maybe they will have a solution for you."

"I hope so, Jay," June added.

Saturday came around slowly, but we got an early start at around 11 a.m. in case we had trouble finding their office. We were a half hour early so we waited in their lobby until June was ushered into a private room. A nurse took her information so they would have some basis to know how to treat her. While in the lobby, I read a lot of their literature showing pictures of various hair transplants. I would come to find out that that was their specialty. They started at $20,000 and went higher.

Later, both June and I were ushered into a large examination room where the doctor examined June's hair and scalp thoroughly. He impressed us a lot. The first thing he said was "June, you are not a candidate for a hair transplant, but I think we can help you."

We both listened to the doctor as he brought out a helmet-like device that looked like something construction workers use. This device was to be used for about twenty minutes after June shampooed her hair. The hard hat, he explained, "has lasers built into it that are designed to stimulate the growth of hair follicles." The doctor put it on June's head to demonstrate it.

The helmet actually talks to the user to tell them what is happening during a twenty-minute treatment. I spoke up to say, "Looks like something you might see on *Star Wars*."

Everyone laughed a little, and June asked the doctor, "Will this really help me?"

"I think it could. We've had a lot of success with it, especially if you use this special shampoo and conditioner before putting on the helmet."

They said the price for the laser helmet was only $970, and they would ship it to us right away. I was happy to pay it, and I said, "If this works, it will be well worth the money."

After the appointment, June and I went around the corner to a nearby restaurant on the plaza and had something to eat before heading back to Kitty Mansion.

Both June and I were very hopeful that we had done something really positive for her hair problem. As we were driving home, June said, "Jay, thanks for helping me get something going on my hair. I feel like we have made real progress, and my hair doctor was really great. I can't wait for the helmet to get here to get started."

"Me too, sweetheart. With the special shampoo and conditioner we purchased and the laser helmet, I think it might have a chance of working. If not, I know of some the guys that might want to rent it from us anyway."

When the helmet arrived a few days later, almost every night when I got home from work, June was wearing it and we both got a laugh when it barked out instructions. I'm not sure how much it helped, but at least we had professional help with June's hair problem and June felt it was helping as well.

CHAPTER 23

MORE BOTTLE FLU

Other than a few AA meetings June attended with her dad, we had not been able to persuade her to get with any outpatient alcohol addiction program available locally. June needed the structure that a program would have. About a month after our trip to Bosley's in Kansas City, I woke up to the sounds of June vomiting in the master bedroom's toilet. This had been happening all too often lately.

I waited until she was through and coming back to ask her, "Are you all right, sweetheart?" I asked.

"I guess," she responded, but I heard her up several more times over the next two hours.

When I did get up, I noticed that she had brought a large plastic trash can with a liner in it next to her side of the bed. I looked at the liner, and I could see that it was almost full, so while she was sleeping, I replaced it with a new liner and took the old one outside to our bigger trash container.

While I was getting ready to go to the office, I couldn't help but notice June was vomiting more, so I phoned my office and let my office manager know what was happening. I decided to wait at home until June hopefully improved.

"June," I said, "I think I'll stay here a while to see if you get better. I just can't leave you alone like this."

"Okay," June responded. After about 10 a.m. and several more bouts of projectile vomiting, June said, "Jay, I'm going to pack a few things in a duffle bag so you can take me to the emergency entrance to the hospital. Maybe they can help me."

"I'll get the car out and ready to go, honey," I said as I headed to the garage.

When we got to the hospital, they checked her into the emergency room area fast and immediately gave her something to help reduce the vomiting. One of the emergency room nurses asked June, "How long has it been since your last drink of alcohol, June?"

"About 10 p.m. last night," June responded. I sort of slumped back in my chair when I heard that, because that was when I briefly left to go to the store to buy more stomach medicine, hoping it would stop the vomiting. Most of the rest of that evening I had spent cat-napping in a chair next to her side of the bed. I was trying to help her get back and forth to the bathroom and watch that she did not drink anything but ice water.

One of the hospital doctors who had been on duty when June was here last came in, and looked at her information briefly and said loudly to her, "June, if you do not stop drinking, you will die! Do you understand?"

June softly responded, "Yes, doctor."

After being on IVs for a few hours, they took June down for x-rays. At least the vomiting had stopped. June hadn't been eating much lately, and I was a little puzzled as to where all the vomit had come from. While June was getting her x-rays, I phoned her mother (Leslie) to let her know where we were, and that I would phone her when June was moved to a room. I knew Leslie would finish the job she was on and come right to the hospital. When they took June to a room, I followed closely behind with her belongings.

When they got her to a room, they gave her something to sleep, so I kissed her on the forehead and told her, "Sweetheart, your mother is coming up soon, so I'll leave for the office now, but I'll be back later in the evening."

"Okay, Jay, I love you, and I'll see you then," June responded, faintly.

I resumed my regular early-morning visits to see June before going to the office when the market opened. I was glad I did, because that was when a very good doctor often came in to check on June and I had a chance to ask questions.

He told June, "At this point, the lab results showed very little liver or kidney damage. But if you don't stop drinking, you will surely have liver damage. June, get involved with an alcohol rehabilitation program soon."

After he left to check on other patients, I told June, "Honey, I'm not experienced in any of this, but I know we can't keep coming here every four to six months. Your body just can't stand it, and sooner or later you will do severe damage to your liver that could prove to be fatal."

Right about that time, a couple of nurses came in to help June take a shower and change her bedsheets because she was unable to move around on her own. So nothing concerning alcohol rehab was resolved. June would be here for another three to four days and back again to outpatient physical rehabilitation at the center across the street to learn how to walk again. The only good thing was that while she was in the hospital or at the rehab center, she was not drinking. However at about $2,500 a day, our money would soon dry up.

CHAPTER 24

DP'D

After three weeklong stays at the hospital and three month-long outpatient physical rehabilitation sessions at the Kansas Rehabilitation Center, the bills were piling up. Before any of this happened, June had purchased one of the ObamaCare medical plans, because her restaurant job did not offer any health care plans for their employees. While it was better than having no health insurance at all, it only covered about half of the hospital bill and none of the other bills for things like radiology, doctors, ambulances, among others.

By that time, I knew we were very likely to have more medical bills to come, and I didn't want June to be hopelessly in debt for the rest of her life. She definitely needed to be on a good group medical program soon. This prompted me to call my human resources department at my job to see if there was any way I could add June to my group health insurance plan. I called a lady in that department I had known for some time and explained our situation.

She said, "Jay, we can put June on your plan right now if you guys get married or if you can prove that you have lived together at your residence for at least one year and are domestic partners."

"How do I go about proving that?" I asked.

"You have to submit three different letters that have come to your residence addressed to June in the past year. Then you both have to go before a notary and swear in a statement that June has lived with you at your residence for the past year. Also, Jay, if you get this to me in the next three weeks, since it is late in the year and our enrollment for next year is almost over, I can still start June on our group plan that you are on and start her on January 1st as your domestic partner."

"Thanks, I'll get back to you soon on this," I replied.

When I got home, I told June about my conversation with the lady in my human resources department. June told me, "Jay, as you know, I moved in with you about a year and a half ago, but most of that time I was still using my mother's address for my mail, and I only switched it to our address here at Kitty Mansion a few months ago. I'll see what mail I can find that might show me living here."

Later that night, June came to me and said, "Jay, here are two envelopes that are addressed to me at our address here."

"That's a good start. What if we go to the public library tomorrow and you order something from them that has to be sent to you here at our address?" I asked June.

"Okay," June responded. "That's worth a try."

A week later, June got the books she ordered from the library with our address on the package. June brought it to me and said, "Jay, this looks like what we need."

"Sure does, sweetheart. I'll get these three things over-nighted to my human resources department with our sworn statement we did before a notary tomorrow morning," I replied.

A few weeks later, we got new health insurance cards for both June and myself, and as I gave her her card, I said, "Sweetheart, we need to go out and have a big dinner to celebrate the fact that an insurance company says that we are officially domestic partners."

"Let's do it soon, Jay," June said as she gave me a big hug and kiss.

We both shouted, "We're now DP'd!"

CHAPTER 25

RACHEL PLATTEN CONCERT

After June was about to finish her third outpatient physical therapy at the Kansas Rehabilitation Center, I spotted an article in the newspaper saying that one of our favorite singers, Rachel Platten, was doing a concert in Lawrence, Kansas, in a few weeks. This concert was to be in an old theater across the street from one of our favorite dining places in Lawrence, the Eldridge Hotel.

I showed the article to June and asked her, "Honey, would you like to go to this concert?"

"Sure," she responded, "if we can still get tickets."

"Here's one of my credit cards. Why don't you call them tomorrow morning and try to get us booked in?" I told her.

"Okay, Jay, I'll call first thing tomorrow morning," June answered excitedly. I was hoping that this would be a really good break for the both of us from the repeated hospital stays and long physical rehabilitation sessions.

About midmorning the next day, June called, "Jay, we are really lucky to get two of the last available seats."

"That's great, sweetheart, and after the concert we can go right across the street and have a steak dinner at the Eldridge too."

"That's a deal," June replied.

The concert was due to start at 6:30 p.m. on a Thursday evening. We got there a half-hour early, but the line to get into the theater was a block long, so we got parked and in line as fast as we could. The theater would only hold twenty-five hundred people, and it was overflowing, but somehow we got pretty good seats in the first balcony.

They had two different warm-up groups ahead of Rachel and her group that were really great on their own. After about an hour, Rachel and her back-up singers and band came on to a thunderous applause. The acoustics in the theater were such that it was hard for me to hear what June was saying, and she was sitting next to me. Rachel and her group were really great. They performed all of the songs on her album and concluded the performance with the two songs she is most known for, "Stand by You" and "Fight Song." She literally brought down the house with those two songs, and she came back out for at least two curtain calls before it was finally over. Needlessly to say, after the concert was over, we waited in line to purchase her album.

When June and I got over to the Eldridge for a late dinner, I told June, "I haven't been to a concert for a long time, but that was really awesome. Didn't you think?"

"Jay, I just loved her song titled 'Fight Song.' I think that song is going to be a favorite song for me now because, as you know, I'm currently in a fight right now with my alcohol addiction."

"Sweetheart, in that case, I'm going to adopt her song 'Stand by You' as my favorite." We then toasted that together with our water glasses.

Our trip to the concert went very well. It was a good break for us both. However, still looming over us was June's out-of-control alcohol addiction problem. Her fight was still ongoing, and we both knew it.

CHAPTER 26

HEAVY DRINKING AGAIN

It wasn't long after June's third hospital stay and month-long outpatient physical rehab at the Kansas Rehabilitation Center that June started drinking heavily every day. June was fairly athletic in high school and even played on her women's basketball team, but the continuous heavy drinking had taken a toll on her body. Whenever she went to her mother's house for the evening, I would search her bedroom and adjoining bathroom area and almost always found and threw away several large bottles of vodka. I even went to the only nearby liquor store in the area with a picture of June and warned them not to sell her more liquor.

The owner told me, "We knew something was wrong and refused to sell her more liquor several months ago."

I told him, "June is nearing a life-or-death situation, and I hope you never sell her anything again."

He said they wouldn't. I had to go to work five days a week and couldn't be around to stop her from getting more alcohol. Where she got her liquor is still a mystery to me.

I wanted June to go back to college and finish her final year since we first met. Her mom and dad wanted her to get some kind of job. Nothing made sense until she stopped drinking. One good thing we had going for us now that we didn't have before is I had recently been able to put June on my health insurance. Now she had good medical, dental, and vision coverage. She never had had this level of coverage, and I kept her busy going to doctors and dentists and professional psychiatrists. It had been a long time since June had had regular medical visits like this unless she was in the hospital. This was of some comfort to me.

Before things got too bad again, I talked to her about going to Valley Hope Rehabilitation Center in Atchinson, Kansas. This center was strongly recommended by the ladies who talked to her while she was in the hospital. June was very reluctant. I'm sure she knew that if she were there, her source of alcohol would be cut off. But she would instead be getting all sorts of addition therapy and counseling daily, not just twice a week. After thoroughly checking it out with my insurance company, they assured me that Valley Hope was an in-network provider and that most of the days at Valley Hope would be covered.

June knew I had been checking around. I came home from work early one day, hoping to catch June while she was still sober. "June," I said, "I checked with our insurance company and with Valley Hope, and it looks like, in maybe a week or two, there might be an opening for you, and it would be mostly covered by our insurance."

June was silent and shaking a little. Even though June had been through some very difficult times, she rarely cried, but I could see a few tears streaming down her cheeks. In a soft and feeble voice, June replied, "Jay, I really don't want to go."

"Sweetheart, the doctors think that you may very well be in the process of destroying your liver and kidneys, and if that happens, you will die," I responded. "June, they have already told us that you can't get in line for a liver or kidney transplant unless you are sober for at least six months. Right now you can't manage one single day sober unless you're in the hospital. June, your mother has been saying all along that you need to be in rehab right now, and I think she is right."

"Jay, I just don't want to go," June responded.

"June, the program at Valley Hope is a voluntary program. They don't force you to be there or force you to stay, but for it to benefit you, you should want to be there and participate in their program." I added, "Sweetheart, even though you have a world-class therapist, he can't be expected to solve your six years of alcohol addiction and heavy drinking with just two sessions a week. You're due to see him next week. Why don't you ask him if he feels it would be good for you to go to Valley Hope for a thirty-day rehabilitation program?"

"I will Jay, but after I had to leave college, I went to two different rehab places and neither one of them helped me at all," June stated. "June, this center has helped a lot of people, and it's totally voluntary. The way they do their program, you can walk away after the first week. The Atchinson facility is only one hour away, and I'll be up there in the evening three to four times a week, so it's not like we would be totally apart for a month," I added.

June and I sat there in silence for, what seemed like, a long time. Finally, June said, "I'll bring it up with Shane in our next session."

"Sweetheart, I get the feeling that if we don't do this or something like it soon, you're not going to make it. I can't stand the thought of you not making it."

I had made my case for June going to rehab, but so far she was not buying into it. Although the hospital stays and outpatient physical rehabilitation sessions temporarily helped June, all we were doing was delaying the inevitable liver and kidney damage and running up big bills at the hospital and physical rehabilitation center. In a few months, we were back where we started with June at home most of the time, drinking her days away and unable to go back to finish her college or go to work.

A few days after we argued about June going to Valley Hope, I was driving her to Shane's for her normal twice-a-week session. "Remember, June, we agreed that you would ask Shane what he thinks about you going to Valley Hope for a month," I reminded her.

"I will, Jay, since it means that much to you," June responded.

When I picked June up after her session, I asked her, "What did Shane say about Valley Hope?"

"He said that he had heard good things about them, and he thinks it would be good for me, but I still don't want to go," June responded.

"June, I know that you are drinking heavy again, and I know something has to change soon before you totally ruin your liver and kidneys for good. We need to get out in front of your addiction problem for a change," I responded.

The drive home was without much other conversation. We had come to an impasse. June had become more homebound as time went by, and except for an occasional trip with me to the store or to her mom's for an evening or an afternoon movie with her dad, she rarely left the house. I think she was at home a lot to drink and protect her various stashes of vodka. She often tried to fix something for us to eat in the evening, but much of the time she wasn't able to do that, so I brought home fast food to make sure she ate something. Even though I tried to get June to watch a movie with me in the evening, June was falling into an alcohol morass that she could not get out of, and I knew of no way I could help her anymore. She could barely make it to the bathroom without help. Often I would go to work for an hour or two and come back home to be with her to try to get her to eat some food, because she had mostly stopped eating. This was different from her previous episodes.

One night, when I got home after work, June was still lying in bed, like she was when I left for work seven hours ago. "June," I said, "I think something is seriously wrong with you. I can't get you to eat much or hardly drink any water, and you aren't responding to much I say anymore."

"Jay," she faintly said, "the way I feel, I really don't care if I live anymore."

"Honey, don't say that," I responded with my voice cracking a little. "Don't you remember all the good times we had?" I added as I held her in my arms. "You have drunk yourself into a stupor, and you really need to go to the hospital now."

"I'm not going anymore," June said defiantly.

"Honey, I've seen a few people die, and you look to me like there's a real possibility you could be dying. Let's go to the hospital while you still can under your own power," I urged her again.

"I'm not going," June stated again.

After June fell asleep, I went downstairs and called June's mom, Leslie, to see if she could come over and talk June into going to the hospital. Since it was late in the evening, Leslie said she would come over early the next morning. I was hoping she could make it right then because I wasn't sure June could make it through the night.

I needed to call Shane to cancel June's appointment. After leaving him a message a few times, he called back. "Shane," I said, "June is close to being comatose with her drinking, and she talks and acts like she has given up. Needless to say, she won't be able to make it to tomorrow's appointment. I've tried to get her to drink some water or soup, but she won't do that either. She needs to go to the hospital, but she won't go."

"Jay," Shane said very directly, "if you don't get her to the hospital soon, she will surely die. Do you understand, it's up to you," Shane said emphatically.

"I'll do my best, Shane," I replied as we both hung up. It was late, but I called my operations manager at his home to let him know I wouldn't make it in to work, at least in the morning and maybe all day. I couldn't sleep, so I put a chair next to June's bed and stayed there through the night until June's mother arrived the next morning.

Early the next morning, the phone downstairs rang and I raced to answer it. It was Leslie, and she asked, "How is June doing?"

"She's still alive, but extremely weak and still saying she won't go to the hospital. Leslie, if she doesn't go to the hospital soon, I'm afraid she's not going to make it," I added.

"Jay, I'll get dressed real quick and come over right away," Leslie answered.

"I'll be sitting next to her bed, so I'll leave the front door unlocked for you to come right in and up to her room," I replied.

When I hung the phone up, I rushed back upstairs. June was half awake by then, so I tried to get her to drink some water.

"Jay," she said faintly, "I don't want anything, I just want to be left alone!"

"Sweetheart, I can't leave you alone. If I do, you will die here maybe today, and I'd never forgive myself. Please don't do this to us. I wouldn't do this to you. You need to go to the hospital now!" I stated resolutely. June just looked away. Nothing I was saying to her was working.

About that time, June's mother came into her room, so I went out into the hallway so Leslie could talk to her privately. When Leslie came out, she was shaken, and I knew she now realized what I told her last night on the phone: that June was near death. Leslie stated several times again that June needed to be in rehab.

"Leslie," I said, "I have cleared the way with Valley Hope for June to go, but she refuses. Now we have another problem. She is physically unable and desperately needs to be in the hospital right now!"

Leslie went back into June's room again and prayed at her bedside. When she came back out, she told me, "June says she wants to stay where she is and die rather than go to the hospital, Jay. Where is your phone downstairs?"

"I'll take you, Leslie," I responded. "I've got an idea for someone to call to see if he can come over and talk to June to get her to go to the hospital," Leslie told me as she dialed the phone.

I went back to June's room while Leslie was talking on the phone. As Leslie came back upstairs, I joined her in the hallway.

"Jay," she said, "help is on the way."

"I'm going back into her room, but you might want to go outside and wait for them to get here. I'll keep talking to her."

"Okay," I said, hoping that maybe we were going to make some progress soon.

In about twenty minutes, two vehicles pulled into our driveway. When they got out, I immediately recognized the pastor of June's church. This had been her pastor since she was born, and June had told me that when she turned sixteen, he had even given her her first car. June and her mother knew the pastor very well. Leslie knew that the pastor was very special to June. If anyone could convince her to go to the hospital, it would be him. I directed the pastor to Leslie and June. I don't know what was said, but Leslie came out first and declared that June had agreed to go to the hospital. Leslie went back into June's room to help her get something on so she could go. At that point, June was unable to move around well enough to get down the stairs, so Leslie and I scooted her down the stairs on her bottom one step at a time. When we got to the last step, three of us carried her to my car for me to drive her to the hospital. I let them go ahead to the emergency room entrance so that they would be waiting with a medic and a wheelchair to get her inside.

CHAPTER 27

LONG HOSPITAL STAY

When we got to the hospital, June was barely responsive to anything anyone said to her. She was mostly comatose. During our trip to the hospital, I tried to get her to talk to me a little, but she was in a daze. When we got to the emergency room, one of the first things the emergency room doctor asked was, "When was the last time you drank any alcohol?"

When June didn't answer, I spoke up and said, "It would have been at least two days, because I've been with her during most of those days I think she is out of alcohol to drink and unable to get more."

During the past few days while June was sleeping, I searched her room and bathroom and threw away what little alcohol I could find that was left. The nurses, as always, put June on IVs and took her to get x-rayed. There were several women from June and her mother's church waiting to get some word from the hospital doctors on how she was doing. This was definitely different from the last three hospital stays, because June could barely respond to anything the nurses or doctors said or did. In short, we needed a miracle for June to come back to life and start to recover. Everyone was praying for that miracle.

They had taken a lot of blood and x-rays while June was still out of it, and the initial results would be coming back soon. After being in the emergency room for about three hours, one of the hospital doctors took Leslie and I aside and said, "June has acute kidney failure and total liver failure. It's possible she may not survive. If she does survive, it's highly likely she has permanently damaged her liver and will develop cirrhosis, and most people eventually die from that condition. We'll do the very best we can to help bring her around, but I cannot guarantee anything at this point." Then he went on to ask, "Who, between the two of you, is the next of kin, and if necessary, if she does not respond to treatment, can authorize us to stop treatment?"

Leslie slowly raised her hand and said, "Doctor, I guess I am. I'm her mother, but I am praying it doesn't come to that." June was Leslie's only child, and since day one she had done everything possible to help her daughter. I knew that it must have been extremely difficult for her to say that.

For the next few days, I spent all of the time that ICU would allow me to in a chair by June's bedside, even though she was barely conscious most of that time. When I came to see June early in the morning on the fourth day, she managed a faint smile. Let me tell you, a smile from June lights up my whole world and then some. This is a gal who has gone through a lot and could still smile a little now and then.

"I like your spirit, sweetheart," I said as I leaned over to kiss her forehead.

"Have you been here long?" she asked faintly.

"I was here a lot of the last three days, sweetheart, and I wanted to be here when you came to," I replied.

The morning of the following day, after June had regained her consciousness and could understand what doctors were telling her, a hospital doctor came in to tell her what they had found.

"June," he said, "due to your heavy drinking, your kidney and liver are in very bad shape. Your bilirubin score is over fifty, which means your liver is severely damaged and almost not working. We are also closely monitoring your kidney function, because every indication we have is that you have acute kidney failure as well." He went on to say, "We are going to be coming in here a lot for blood work so we can see if you have had any improvement."

June managed a faint, "Okay, Doctor. Thank you," before he left. I was glad that I had been there when the doctor told June of her condition, so that there was no misunderstanding the severity of her problems this time. After the nurse took June's blood again, June told me, "Jay, I think I would like to try to sleep a little before I have a lot of visitors. Can you ask one of the nurses if they could bring me something to help me sleep on you way out?"

"Sweetheart, I'll do that and later tonight, after most of your visitors have left. I'll be back." With that said, I bent over, kissed her on the forehead, and left for the office.

While June was somewhat better and at least coherent, she was far from being well enough to be able to get up and have someone walk her up and down the hallway as they had before. This hospital stay was going to be much longer. After being in the hospital for about a week, the doctors were still saying that June's kidney and liver were still in the acute failure zone. Nothing the doctors were doing was working yet. This time June's body was not responding to treatment, but at least it wasn't getting any worse. I mostly sat by her bed and held her hand while she alternated back and forth between being conscious and asleep.

Two weeks of this went by with only a little improvement. I have been told that her liver will regenerate and heal itself, but June's improvement was going very slowly, if at all. At least she was now coherent most of the time and could speak in a soft voice. June, however, was now able to eat some solid food. And the hospital physical therapy people were coming in daily helping June do some exercises and walk a little with help. This gave me some hope.

During this hospital stay, June had been in ICU all of the time, which somewhat restricted the visiting hours. Knowing that June would probably be discharged in a few weeks, the hospital assigned a liver specialist to continue working with her while she was still there and after she was to be discharged. June's liver problems continued to persist and were still in the life-threatening category. The liver doctor's nurse practitioner was very good and worked directly with June. She and June became friends, but she used special blood tests to determine if June was still drinking after her release from the hospital.

When June was about to be released, she was visited again by two social workers who urged her to get involved with either various local or regional inpatient or outpatient alcohol treatment facilities. We promised to make an effort to check these out this time.

At the end of the third week, June was released again from the hospital. Like the last time, she was directed to go to the same physical rehabilitation center she had been going to before, starting the very next week.

CHAPTER 28
FINAL HOSPITAL STAY

After June spent over three weeks in the hospital and another month and a half at the physical rehabilitation center on an outpatient basis, she was functioning more or less normally. We had been told that she would likely be in outpatient care for her liver, maybe for years, because she still had a very high bilirubin score. She was assigned a very good nurse practitioner named Lea to work with her. At first she had appointments at least weekly with special blood tests on a weekly basis. Until June could show she could go without drinking for a reasonable period, I didn't feel it was the right time for her to go back to school or work. There might be too much pressure with her doing either one.

With her various visits with Lea for her liver, and her therapy sessions with Shane and another psychologist, she was somewhat busy. In the back of my mind, I knew we should be in inpatient care for her alcohol addiction, but June kept being noncommittal about that. After several special blood tests and visits to Lea, I asked June, "What is Lea saying about your liver?"

"She tells me that my liver is still not functioning very well and that she wants to monitor my liver weekly for now, but she has arranged for me to get special liver pills for free that are normally very expensive," June replied.

"Sweetheart, I want to do everything we can so that you can get better. I know that there are no guarantees in life, but I don't want to leave anything to chance. You are too precious to me," I responded.

June paused for a few moments while she fought back a tear and said in a soft voice, "Sweetheart, what you have done for me is more than anyone has ever done, but the alcohol addiction problem I have is hard to beat. I don't want you to get your hopes up." I wanted it to be a fun evening, so I let that conversation lapse for now.

Unfortunately, she was indeed still drinking. Lea's liver blood tests proved it. I was beside myself trying to figure out how and where she was getting the vodka, but she was getting it in sizable quantities. With her liver already in a very questionable state, I knew that practically any amount of drinking could possibly cause her fatal results. The only thing June was doing for alcohol rehab was going with her dad, a longtime reformed alcoholic, to an occasional AA meeting.

"June," I asked, "what are you going to do to stop this vicious cycle you are in with your drinking?"

"Jay," she replied, "I don't really know, but in the end it will probably take care of itself."

"Sweetheart, at my age I try not to be afraid of things in my life, but your drinking has me terrified. You have been warned by all of your many doctors and nurses over the past three years that if you keep drinking you will die. If you die here at Kitty Mansion, then I'll die here of a broken heart too. Can't you see that?"

June did not respond.

A few weeks later, on a Saturday morning, I went into June's room to see how she was doing. I tried talking to her, but she was very incoherent. I could see she was becoming comatose again. I knew that I needed to do something soon or she could die, maybe that very day. I had no time left now to call others to talk to her. She was too far gone. I quickly went downstairs and called for an ambulance to take her to the hospital. When the ambulance arrived and loaded June up, I called Leslie and let her know we were headed to the hospital again. Leslie said she would meet us there. We were both very familiar with the hospital routine by that time.

It took a few days at the hospital in ICU before June was coherent again. I literally stayed by her side holding her hand a lot of that time. Like Rachel's song said, "I'm going to stand by her" all the way. After June went through her normal withdrawal period, I resumed my regular visits early in the mornings and then back later in the evening after most of the other visitors had left for the day. After about a week into this stay, June was able to converse with people normally.

Early one morning, about two weeks into this hospital stay when I came to visit June, she seemed excited about what the head nurse on her evening shift had to say about the Valley Hope Rehabilitation Center in Atchinson, Kansas.

"Jay, I know that I have resisted going to rehab before, but this nurse recently went through the program with her son that had a drinking problem like me, and it sounds really good. I have arranged for her to come back later tonight to tell you about it."

"Sweetheart, that's great, I'm anxious to hear all about it."

"It sounds like just the right program for me when I get out of here," June added. "Having someone with recent firsthand experience with that program would be great to hear," I responded.

I arranged to be back to the hospital after 8:00 p.m. Soon after that time, the head nurse in charge of that shift in June's area came into her room. She started by telling us that the Valley Hope program at Atchinson, Kansas, had been very instrumental in helping her son through his alcohol and substance abuse problems.

She went on to say, "The way the program was set up, I was able to go to several of the meetings with my son. During the thirty-day period that most people are in the program, they have at least five meetings that the whole family can attend to help the family understand and deal with the problems their loved one has been having," she added. She went on to say, "The men are in a men's dormitory with two men to each room, and the women in a separate area with two women sharing each room. Much like a college dormitory. During the day, they mostly have group meetings everyone attended, but they also have private sessions almost every other day with each participant," she pointed out. "Later in the evening, they often load everyone up in the cars of different instructors and counselors and go to a regular AA meeting. This is so people get used to going to meetings regularly," she added.

After the nurse left, June said, "Jay, after I learn to walk again on my own at Kansas Rehabilitation Center, I think the program at Valley Hope is what I should do. Don't you?"

"Sweetheart, finally I think we are on the right track to solving your alcohol problem. You have been here in this hospital five times over the past two years. The last two times you almost died before we got you here. Going to Valley Hope at Atchinson, Kansas, seems like the right thing for you to do. I'll start talking to them again after you get out of here," I added.

"Jay, I think I'm ready to go, but don't say anything to my parents for now. I want to surprise them."

"I'll let it come from you," I replied.

It took at least another week for June's liver and kidney to stabilize enough to where she could go to outpatient physical rehab so she could learn to walk on her own again. After this three-week hospital stay, I was able to take her back to Kitty Mansion. This time, things were different. We both had agreed on a strong plan to help her with her alcohol addiction. We both felt hopeful.

CHAPTER 29

GETTING READY FOR ALCOHOL REHAB

From the moment June was released from the hospital until the time she started her usual physical rehab at Kansas Rehabilitation Center so she could walk again on her own, I was apprehensive. I knew it would take at least a month or two of physical rehab before she would be in good enough physical condition to go to Valley Hope, and I didn't want her to start drinking again before she could get there. I had been told that Valley Hope is a detox facility to start with for everyone. I didn't want June needing to spend very many days in detox before she was allowed to go into their alcohol rehabilitation program.

While June's kidneys and liver were somewhat better, she was still in the failure zone. The medications and constant meetings with her doctors, nurses, and therapists were helping, but I felt like we were walking a tightrope until we could get to Valley Hope and get round-the-clock care for her. Shane, her main therapist, strongly supported her decision to go to Valley Hope. June seemed now to be in agreement.

"Sweetheart," I said to June, "I'm glad you're onboard with going to Valley Hope as soon as you can walk again. We have to do something different this time. I don't think you can do another hospital stay."

"Jay, all my doctors are saying the same thing, so let's get it on as soon as we can," June responded. That next day, I began preliminary discussions again with Valley Hope in Atchinson.

A few weeks later, June and I decided we would go to the Sunday morning service at June's church. Before we got there, June reminded me, "Jay, don't say anything to my folks or anyone about me going to Valley Hope. I want to surprise them."

"Sweetheart, I won't. I want it to be your present to them," I responded.

The pastor gave a really inspiring sermon, and after church at least a dozen people gathered around June wanting to know how she was doing. Many of the same people had visited June often during her hospital stays. I just stood back while June visited with them. Many of these people had known June all of her life and were very happy to see that June was doing better.

After June had been in physical rehab about a month, she felt that she was ready to go to alcohol rehab at Valley Hope. "Jay," she said, "why don't you call the admissions people at Valley Hope and see how soon I can start?"

I did, and I reported back to June, "They say that they have an opening next Monday morning, and they can start processing you in at 9 a.m."

"Good," June responded. "I'm going to pack a small satchel with some essentials and when you come up to visit me, if I need anything else, you can bring it then. In the information they sent us, they said they have laundry facilities."

That next Monday morning we were up early to leave for Valley Hope in Atchinson, Kansas. Before we left town, June asked me to stop at her mother's house because she wanted to tell her the good news. When we got to her mother's, I said, "June, you go in alone to give her the good news, and I'll wait in the car."

After we got to Valley Hope and went through an hour-long in-processing, June turned to me, gave me a big farewell hug and kiss, and said, "Jay, they are putting me in a detox ward for one to three days to determine exactly how I'm doing. So I won't be able to call you 'til I get out of there."

As they were leading June away, I said, "Sweetheart, call me as soon as you can, I love you."

June responded with "Jay, I love you right back."

CHAPTER 30

GETTING STARTED AT
VALLEY HOPE

After they took June away, I drove back to my office in Topeka to try to get in at least three hours of work that afternoon. I was hoping that working would maybe help me get over them leading June away because I knew it would be at least three days before I would see her again. When I got to the office, my operations manager asked me, "How did it go, Jay?"

"I guess it went as good as it could, considering she will be there about a month and I'm not used to her being gone that long," I responded. "When she gets out of the detox ward, I will at least be able to go there a few evenings a week and back again on a Saturday or Sunday afternoon," I added. "This is something she has been needing to do since I first started going with June and realized after six months that she had a severe alcohol addiction problem. I hope it works because it may be our last chance to get her to stop drinking. Her life literally depends on it."

"I hope it works too," he responded as he handed me at least a dozen phone calls for me to answer that afternoon. He went on to say, "The call from Jimmy is a priority. He's really upset that his account isn't beating the S&P this year."

"Well, Jimmy, has an account that Warren Buffet would like to have. He started with fourteen thousand fifteen years ago and we made several great trades together and now it's worth over half a million dollars. For the last two years he's become very defensive and won't invest more than one-third to one half of his money at any given time with the rest of his money in a money market getting one-tenth of 1 percent. And what's worse is when a stock we have bought goes up a point or two, he takes a small profit, instead of letting his profits ride. Well you know what they say, 'Scared money never wins.' I'll call him right away."

Two days later at work, I got my first phone call from June.

"Jay," she said, "I'm out of detox, and tomorrow I'm going to be starting my meetings. From what I can see, they are going to be really good."

"That's great, sweetheart," I responded. "When can I come up to visit you?" I asked.

"I'm glad you asked that," June said, "because tomorrow night at six they are having a group meeting just for friends or family of patients. Can you come to that?"

"You bet I'll be there," I responded. "I can't talk long, but I'll be waiting for you in the parking lot a little before six tomorrow night. Love you," June said as she hung up.

The next day at work seemed like it was going slow, but I managed to get through it and promptly left work at three just after the market closed. I raced home to Kitty Mansion to feed the kitties and pack a few clothes June asked me to bring. I got to Valley Hope just before my first group meeting, and June was waiting for me in the parking lot.

"Jay, It's really great seeing you," she blurted out while giving me a big hug and kiss. "I've been out here since 5:30, and we don't have much time before your meeting starts," June added.

"I've really missed you too, sweetheart," I replied.

"Take my hand Jay, and I will guide you to your meeting, because it is about to start," June said. "When your meeting is over, I'll show you around," she added.

Just as June said, this meeting was just for family or friends of loved ones who were there for their alcohol or drug abuse problems, not for participants of the program. The staff member who was running the meeting was a young man named Dillon (first name). He was exceptional. He tried to get us all involved by having each of us briefly talk about one thing we had experienced with our loved one who was in the program. After each person spoke, he sometimes made remarks that would help them deal with their loved one in the program. This, I would later find out, was the first of five different sessions, sometimes with other counselors, that were designed to help us understand and deal with our loved one's problems. When it was my turn to speak, he asked me to identify myself and tell something about what my partner was going through.

"I'm Jay Sherrer, and June Burns is my domestic partner. June has had a constant and severe addiction to alcohol since her last year at college almost five years ago. She has been in the hospital five times and almost died twice with acute kidney and liver failure. Valley Hope is the third rehabilitation facility she has been to and we are both hoping that this will do it for her. When June isn't drinking, she is a wonderful person and would literally give anyone that needed it the shirt off of her back."

Dillon thanked me and went on to the next person, but I felt he was likely storing up information to use later on and this was just the initial contact.

After our group meeting was over, June grabbed my hand and showed me around the facility. It looked to me like a very small college campus with a large area like a student union that everyone assembled in before and after their meetings. It had the men's and women's dormitory off of the assembly room and various meeting rooms as well. On the lower level, there was a large kitchen and dining area that sometimes doubled as a meeting room. All in all, I would say, a very functional facility.

At about 7 p.m., most of the group meetings were over, and June had the option of signing out with a sponsor, but she had to be back by 9 p.m. to go to a late AA meeting.

"Have you had dinner yet?" I asked June.

"No, I was waiting for you in the parking lot," June replied.

"Well, I saw a few places when I drove through the downtown area. Let's go check one of them out," I said as June was signing out.

After we found a place that looked like it might be good, during dinner I naturally asked June, "How is it going?"

"Really good. I like my roommate, and the group meetings are something like being back in college. I have a really good lady counselor that is easy to talk to as well."

"Jay, I can tell already that this is a much better alcohol rehabilitation facility than I have been to before."

"Great, sweetheart! I can't tell you how good that is for me to hear. All of the kitties really miss you, but I'll tell them you are doing fine," I added.

When we finished dinner and got back to the facility, I told June, "Remember, call me every day, and I'll try to get back in a few days."

"Okay, Jay, I will. Remember, I love you," June added. We hugged and kissed before she had to go.

CHAPTER 31

MORE VALLEY HOPE

The "friends and family" meetings became more involved to help us get prepared for the time when our loved one was to leave. I made every one of them and asked every question I could think of. While I really missed June, I knew she was finally getting the help she needed by very skilled people. When I came to visit and I looked into June s eyes, I could see that she was literally coming alive again. Her smile was glowing like it never had before. She seemed more confident in herself. The alcohol did not have its terrible grip on her anymore.

June told me, "Jay, when I finish my rehab here, they have emphasized that I need to go to at least ninety AA meetings in ninety days. So I'm going to be going to a lot of meetings."

"Sweetheart, if that is what it takes, then I would urge you to go for it. They have been helping people with their addictions for a long time, and I think that they know what it takes to get better."

After at least ten trips to visit June and attending at least that many meetings myself, it was close to the time that June was to finish her rehab at Valley Hope. I came up to Valley Hope late in the morning on a Sunday to attend June's final meeting with her. She had already packed up her stuff and said goodbye to her roommate.

June said to me, "Jay, this has been a really great month for me. I have made several friends. I have a far greater insight into my addiction problem now than I have ever had before."

"Sweetheart, that's really good for me to hear," I responded.

Before the final meeting was to begin, June took my hand and led me over to someone she wanted me to meet.

"Jay, I want to introduce you to my main counselor, Deedra. I have been meeting with her two to three times a week for the past month She has been a really big help to me."

"Glad to meet you, Deedra," I said while shaking her hand.

"Jay," Deedra said, "June has told me a lot about the help you have given her over the past three years and we feel that she has made a great deal of progress over the past month."

"That's great to hear, Deedra," I responded.

Then later, as the final meeting was coming to an end, several people testified as to their feelings about their month-long stay at Valley Hope. Everyone was then asked to stand and join hands and repeat the "Serenity Prayer."

> God, grant me the serenity to accept the
> things I cannot change, the courage to
> change the things I can and the wisdom
> to know the difference.
>
> (Written by Reinhold Niebular)

CHAPTER 32

NINETY MEETINGS
IN NINETY DAYS

On our drive back to Topeka, June said to me, "Jay, I'm going to need to have both you and my dad drive me to AA meetings every day until I can get at least a restricted driver's license and drive myself. Are you up for it?"

"Sure, I'll do whatever it takes to get you to as many meetings a week as we can," I replied. "Sweetheart, why don't you look into getting one of those breath devices for our car so you can get a restricted license and drive yourself?"

"I'll make some calls tomorrow," June added.

One of the first regular meetings June started to go to was a ladies-only meeting every Saturday morning at 9 a.m. that was held at a large church downtown. When we pulled into the church parking lot for the first time, I remarked to June, "Gee, this is a large parking lot, and it's almost full of cars. There must be a lot of women in Topeka that have or have had alcohol problems."

"Sure seems like it," June responded.

The Saturday morning meeting would become one of June's favorite meetings and a place that she made a lot of close friends too. She hardly ever missed that meeting. I gladly took June every Saturday morning to that meeting. One of the ladies at the Saturday morning meeting who became friends with June invited her to a small meeting every Thursday evening that was called a "book study" group meeting.

June explained to me, "Jay, what they do at that meeting is study, page by page, the AA book like it was a Bible." June went on to say, "Some of those ladies are lawyers or they have PhDs, or they have strong professional backgrounds. So I feel fortunate to be asked to come into their group. Their friendship and support is very helpful to me, Jay."

The official AA meeting place is located in about the middle of town. It's a well-built brick by-level building. It was probably a house at one time. The upper level was converted into one large meeting room. I'm guessing that it would probably hold up to one hundred people. It also has a large blacktopped parking area behind the house. They call it "the Clubhouse." There is a meeting every afternoon at 4:30 p.m. Monday through Saturday for both men and women combined and a very well-attended Sunday morning meeting at 10 a.m. June's dad often would pick up June for the afternoon meeting.

The central point of June's dad's life for most of the past twelve years had been the Clubhouse. After dragging his mother's wallet through twelve different month-long rehabs for alcohol and substance abuse, he finally gained his sobriety twelve years ago. June's mother had divorced him years before because of the terrible influence he had become while June was growing up. There have been numerous articles and probably some books written about the hereditary effects that a mother or father has on a child if that parent is an alcoholic. Often they follow in that parent's footsteps and become alcoholics themselves. I don't know if that was true in June's case, but it certainly didn't help that he was drunk and on drugs much of the time June was growing up. To his credit, however, over the past six years, he stepped back into June's life and tried everything he could to help her overcome her drinking problems. Almost daily, he called her and often invited her to go to AA meetings with him. And since they both liked movies, he often took her to a matinee. At least during those times, June was not drinking.

CHAPTER 33

BICYCLING

Until she could get a restricted driver's license, June decided to take up bicycling. June said to me, "Jay, I need to get a bicycle. If I get good enough, I can even ride my bicycle to some of my meetings."

"Sounds good to me," I responded. "We don't have a lot of extra money right now, but maybe on your birthday, next Saturday, we can go to the main bicycle shop in town and see if they have a good used one we can buy for you to get started with."

"That sounds great to me, Jay," June replied.

When we got to the shop, we were met by a young man named Larry. Larry made us feel at home. He introduced himself and said he was co-owner of what looked to be a sizable shop with lots of new bikes displayed.

June said, "Larry, my name is June, and I'm thinking of taking up bicycling, but I don't know if I will like it so I thought I would start off with a good used bike, but it looks like you only have new ones."

Larry said, "Hold on a minute, I think I might have just the thing for you." Larry disappeared into the back room and reappeared with a bright gold-colored ladies' bike. "June, why don't you take this one out into the large parking lot outside and ride it around to see if you like it?" All three of us went outside and watched June ride. "Hold it a minute," Larry said to June. "I think I can make an adjustment to the height of the seat to make it better for you." After he adjusted the seat, June got back on and rode it some more.

When June came back to the shop, she said, "Jay, I really like it."

"Okay then, let's talk to Larry about buying it."

Larry said, "How did you like it, June?"

"I really liked it, Larry, but I don't know if I can afford it."

"That's the good part, June. We get lots of trade-ins in here so I can make you a special price of $135.00."

I immediately spoke up and said, "We'll take it, Larry." There was money left over to buy a pair of leather bicycling gloves as well.

Almost immediately, June began riding. First, it was just around the block. Then she saw a lot of people riding their bikes around Lake Shawnee, close by our house, so that was next.

June said to me, "Jay, I think the lake is about eight miles around it and I'm going to try to make it clear around the lake by a week from now."

"June, that's a pretty ambitious goal for someone that has been riding for only three days," I responded.

Soon June was going around the lake every day. The bicycle shop we purchased June's bike at emailed her that they were starting a weekly ladies-only group ride every

Wednesday night. They were led by an experienced bicyclist. They took various routes around town every week and usually went at least twenty miles each ride. June didn't stop with that. She joined several groups that rode other nights of the week as well.

Late in the fall, June and another lady bicyclist went to meets in both Lawrence and Kansas City for large bicycle events. They both rode forty miles at each meet. For Christmas, I bought June a good stationary bike that June could use in her room when weather was bad outside. June and I had quite a time putting it together, but it is now a really good thing for her to have during winter months.

It is remarkable what bicycling has done for June's body. I was massaging her sore legs one evening, and in just six months of bicycling, her legs had filled out and were bulging with muscles. I can't help but believe this was having a very positive effect on her kidneys and liver as well.

CHAPTER 34

IGNITION INTERLOCK DEVICE

In the state of Kansas, if you have had a DUI within five years of applying for a restricted driver's license, you have to have an ignition interlock device installed in your car for a period of two years. There are about half a dozen various devices to choose from on the market. Most of the companies that manufacture these devices rent them to you for about $120 a month, and they require you to go back to the dealer that installed the device every month and have it recalibrated for $15 extra. If you don't do the recalibration, the car will not start until you do.

June said to Jay, "I'm going to see who handles these interlock devices and try to arrange for them to install one this Saturday morning, if possible."

"Okay, sweetheart," Jay responded, "It's time for you to be driving again, so see what you can arrange."

A few days later, June reported back. "There is an auto detailing company over by Wannamaker Street that installs and recalibrates these devices as a sideline business. I'll call them and see if they can do it this Saturday."

After calling them, June said to Jay, "They can do it at 10 a.m. this Saturday. Is that okay with you?"

"Let's do it," Jay responded.

When we got there, the auto detailing side of the business was busy with at least three cars lined up and workers detailing them. The owner was named Danny. His uncle Charley was also there helping coordinate the production. Danny was very conversational and an impressive guy. He had a humor about him that made us feel at home almost instantly.

He started out by asking June, "Gal, what can I do for you today?" June recounted her conversation with him from a few days ago about installing the interlock device. "Why don't you guys make yourselves comfortable in the lobby and I'll get the car in and do the installation?"

About a half hour later, Danny came to the lobby and told us that he was done and invited both of us to come out into the garage area where the car was parked so he could demonstrate it to us.

"Gal," Danny said to June, "you sit in the front seat next to me so I can show you how the device works."

Danny blew into the device so that the car would start. It did. Next he had June change seats with him so that June could be in the driver's seat and try to start the car.

"Gal," Danny said to June, "you try it." June did, but it didn't start. June looked puzzled. "Blow harder, gal," Danny instructed her. She did and it finally started. Danny drove the car to a nearby private parking lot in a shopping center that had enough room for both June and I to practice blowing into the device and starting the car. I would be driving the car home until June could get her license, so Danny had me practice blowing into the device several times until I finally got the hang of it.

Once we got back to Danny's shop, he emphasized to June, "Gal, you have to bring the car in before the first of every month for me or Uncle Charlie to recalibrate the device."

"I will," June responded.

The following Monday, I drove the car to the driver's license bureau so they could inspect the car and June could take her driver's test to get her restricted license. June passed both the written and practical test and was rewarded with a restricted driver's license.

As we were leaving, I turned to June and said, "Sweetheart, since I have known you, over the past five years, this is the first time you have been able to drive yourself."

"It's a really great feeling, Jay," June responded.

"Honey," I added, "As Forrest Gump would say, 'One less thing.'"

CHAPTER 35
GOING BACK TO COLLEGE

Until June had to drop out of college in her senior year due to her drinking, she was a straight A student. She was looking to get two degrees, one in philosophy and one in English literature. Working with her counselors at both Washburn University and Seattle Pacific University, June was to take courses in philosophy at Washburn that they would accept at Seattle Pacific to complete her philosophy degree that they would award her there when she passed. Plus, Washburn would give her the remaining English literature courses she needed to complete her English literature degree at Washburn. These were all senior-level courses and would not be easy, especially for someone who has been out of college for over five years.

But June said to me, "Jay, I really like the academic life that exists at college, so I think that studying hard almost every day is what I really want to do. I've broken it up, though, so I'll be finishing my philosophy degree first over the next two semesters with a little English literature for now and when that's over, I'll concentrate on the English literature courses I need to finish that degree."

"Sweetheart, don't overload yourself. You know that you haven't been in college for a while, and these are senior-level classes," I responded.

"I should be okay, Jay," June replied.

One thing that really changed now that June had her restricted driver's license was that June became the main driver of our car and not me. I was being chauffeured almost everywhere, including to the office in the mornings. I really liked that, mainly because I had grown tired of driving all the time. But I told June, "Honey, since I want you to focus on your driving, I think we should give up kissing at Stop signs—at least for now."

"Okay, Jay."

Shortly after June dropped me off one morning, on her way to Washburn, I was to have a meeting with a big client I have mentioned before, JR. I had planned out what I wanted him to do the day before. When he came in, I started by saying, "JR, you have over $250,000 in your money market account that is only drawing one-tenth of one percent interest and that is dragging down the performance of the whole account."

"Jay, just what do you think I should do about that?"

"Since the market is starting to move higher, I think you should get more invested right now," I responded. "I recommend that you buy $50,000 in each of these three stocks: Disney, Honeywell, and JP Morgan-Chase."

JR shot back, "Just why should I buy all of these now?"

"JR, I'm thinking of taking delivery of a new Rolls-Royce Phantom and I could use the commissions," I responded.

"What?" he shouted.

"Hey," I replied, "I'm really just kidding. I still buy my gas $10 at a time, and I really like the Ford I'm driving, but I do think that you will do well in these stocks."

"Okay, Jay, go ahead and buy them," JR said as he was leaving.

CHAPTER 36

PHILOSOPHY DEGREE

In June's quest to complete two degrees, she was now facing two semesters of senior-level philosophy courses. Not an easy assignment for someone who hadn't seen a classroom in over five years—also for someone who was trying to participate in at least one AA meeting almost every day. Since I mentioned AA, at this point in time, June had just received her one-year sobriety coin signifying that she remained sober for one full year. In AA parlance, this marked her one-year birthday. To celebrate this anniversary, June and her mother and father and I went out to dinner together. We had a lot to be thankful for. June's mother led us in prayer before we ate our meal.

"Thank you, Lord, for helping June stay sober this past year and that she is now going back to college and able to drive herself as well. These accomplishments, with your help, have been very big for her. Amen."

When the first semester of philosophy was beginning, June had to take an upper-level course in logic. This course was rooted mainly in mathematics. After a few weeks of logic, June said, "Jay, I have always struggled with upper-level mathematics, and I'm going to need to get some tutoring to help me get through this logic course."

"Sweetheart," I replied, "can you get some extra help from your instructor?"

"I've bothered him enough already," June responded. "Here's what I have worked—out a few of my classmates are having troubles too and we have decided to meet three nights a week at the Washburn library to help each other with all of the logic equations. I'll have to go back to Washburn after I drop you off from work three nights a week, and we will work as late as we need to complete our assignments."

"Honey, I'll get my own dinner on those nights, so do what you need to do to get through that course," I responded.

The semester dragged on, but June kept with it until she finally passed the difficult logic part of her philosophy degree. Even though she only made a B on her logic courses, June still did enough overall on her other philosophy courses on both semesters to complete her degree in philosophy.

A few weeks after completing the courses, June came to me and said "Jay, look what I got in the mail today. My philosophy degree from my old college, Seattle Pacific."

"That's great, sweetheart. Put that in a special place so you can see it every day. Why don't we go out to dinner tonight and celebrate?"

A few days after we celebrated with dinner, June said to me, "Jay, after the summer break is over, I know my main degree, English literature, is waiting for me to finish."

"Sweetheart, I'm confident that with all your knowledge of classical literature, you'll do great with that," I responded.

CHAPTER 37

ROAD TRIP

"Sweetheart, since you passed your driver's test and now have a driver's license and you have a birthday coming up in a few weeks, I think it's time we went on a road trip," I said to June.

"Jay, that sounds great! Just what did you have in mind?" June replied.

"Honey, have you ever heard of the Elms Resort and Spa?" I responded.

"No, I haven't," June replied. "The Elms is in Excelsior Springs, Missouri. That's north of Kansas City about thirty miles and is about a two-hour drive from here. It's an old combination roadhouse/hotel built in the late 1800s. During the roaring '20s, the gangster Al Capone and his gang used to come down to Kansas City and stayed at the Elm's so he could play cards with his Kansas City gangster buddies. And both presidents Truman and Roosevelt frequently stayed there too."

"Really?" June stated. "That sounds really interesting."

"Years ago, I took my ex-wife there, and she really enjoyed it. I think you would like it too," I replied. "The food is really great, and they have an indoor pool and spa and live entertainment on Saturday nights as well."

"Sounds like a lot of fun to me. I'm finishing my last philosophy class in a few weeks, so let's go right after that," June responded.

"Sweetheart, I'll book us in for two weeks from now for a Friday and Saturday night, and I'll take off early from work that Friday night so we can get there well before dinner."

"Jay," June said, "since there is an indoor pool and spa, we both will need new bathing suits. Our existing suits are really old."

"Honey, here's a hundred dollars. I'll put you in charge of that while I make the reservations," Jay responded.

A day later, I reported to June, "I've booked a one-bedroom suite for two weekends from now overlooking the river running by the hotel."

Since June was now our official driver, I took over the duties of our navigator. I put extra food out for our kitties early that Friday afternoon before we left Kitty Mansion for the Elm. As we approached the Elm, the area close to the hotel is somewhat hilly and just before we got there, we pulled to the side of the road to see a beautiful view of it about six blocks down below.

"Sweetheart, that's where we are headed. Doesn't that look great?" I told June.

"It really does," June responded.

After we parked, I got in line to check us in while June looked over the large lobby area. When we got to the room, we unloaded our stuff and headed to the main dining room to try to beat the crowd. Dinner was great.

After dinner, I said to June, "Why don't we go to our suite and get into our bathing suits and go down to the pool and spa area and see what they have?"

"Sounds great to me," June replied. The hotel provided us with robes to wear to the pool and spa area.

When we got there, it wasn't that crowded, so June said, "I'm going into the pool first while not many people are in the pool yet, so why don't you join me, Jay?"

"I'll join you in a few minutes, but I'm going to see if I can book us a couple's massage for tomorrow night," I replied.

When I got back to the pool area, I told June, "Honey, it was good. I went in to book a couple's massage because they were almost booked up for the weekend. They told me that in the future we should book the massages when we make our reservations because they get booked up really quickly on the weekend. However, they had a cancellation for 8 p.m. tomorrow night, so I took it."

"That's great, Jay," June responded. "Now get in the pool with me, the water is fine."

After sloshing around in the pool, both June and I took to the steam room and hit the showers before heading back to the suite to order up a movie and falling asleep watching it while holding each other. The end of a great day.

On Saturday, we both slept late and enjoyed the fruit basket left in our room before going down to the main dining room for a late breakfast. At breakfast, I said to June, "Honey, I think they have a free tour of this historic place we are in. Would you like to go?

"Sure, Jay. It sounds like it would be very interesting," June replied.

That afternoon, we joined about a dozen other guests taking the tour. The lady leading our tour first took us to a large room above the front entrance and said, "This is where Al Capone and his gang played cards with his Kansas City gangster friends when he visited. You can see that there are several holes in the baseboard facing the front entrance for machine guns to be used if a rival gang or federal officers made a raid."

Also she took us upstairs to two large suites. In the first one, she said, "This is called the Truman Suite and is named after President Truman." Then we went to a larger suite on the top floor. "This is called the Roosevelt Suite, named after President Roosevelt," she said. She went on to point out, "He needed a larger area because he was in a wheelchair most of the time. President Roosevelt visited the Elm a lot to soak his body in hot natural mineral water baths that Excelsior Springs was known for."

Later that evening, after a great dinner, June and I changed back in into our bathing suits to go back to the pool and spa and steam room before our couple's massage.

After the massage, I told June, "What a great way to end our trip."

"Jay, I think the whole trip has been great, and I'm glad we came."

As we were checking out Sunday morning, a very skilled pianist was playing a very lively selection of Jerry Lee Lewis songs on a grand piano and invited anyone who wanted to join in and sing along with him.

"June what a great way to end our trip," I said.

CHAPTER 38
ENGLISH LITERATURE DEGREE

In late August, June was scheduled to start the first of two semesters of advanced English literature courses to finish her English literature degree at Washburn University. If she passed, this degree would be awarded by Washburn. June said to me, "Jay, I need to do really well over the next two semesters to make high grades in order to be admitted to Kansas University's graduate program." She went on to say, "I'll be studying at the Washburn library late at night a lot."

"June," I replied, "I understand that you have a lot to do, so I'll let you tell me when you have time for me and the kitties."

The first semester went well, but during that time she had at least three five- to ten-page papers to write in addition to try to keep up with her AA meetings. One of the positive things June had going for her was her professors.

"Jay," June said, "This semester's classes are being taught by really good professors that require great things from their students but really help you get there too. I know that if I'm having trouble with something, they are there to help."

The first semester's work was extensive, but when it was over June said, "Look, Jay, I got all As. I can't wait to show my mom."

"Good for you, sweetheart. Why don't we all go out for dinner?"

After the break for the holidays, June's final semester started. It became clear fairly soon that her main final English literature course was going to be judged by a ten-page essay she was to write, after reading several books.

June said, "Jay, the lady professor teaching this course is really good, so to make things interesting, she is holding an essay-writing contest and the winning student will be allowed to present their essay at a small symposium in a few weeks. I'm going to try very hard to win that contest."

At the end of the two weeks, when June was picking me up after work, she said, "Guess what, Jay! I won the essay contest."

"That's wonderful, sweetheart. I know that you worked extra hard on that," I said as I gave her a big hug.

After a very professional presentation at the symposium, June's final semester was over and grades were in and again June posted straight As to complete her English literature degree.

CHAPTER 39

GRADUATION

This year's graduation ceremony is being held in the Washburn sports area. Over four hundred students are being awarded various degrees. I got seated down as close to the floor level as I could because I intended to get on the floor when June was being presented her degree so I could take pictures. At the podium was the chancellor of the university. He would be calling out each student's name and the degree they were being awarded. Behind him were various PhDs and department heads who were awarding degrees. The stage was set.

As all of the students who were getting degrees filed into the area, wearing their caps and gowns, I was able to pick out June about halfway in the large group. After they were seated, a local dignitary gave a thirty-minute graduation address challenging the students to go forth and make life better for themselves and others.

After the address was over, the chancellor began calling out the names of each student being awarded a degree to come forward and be presented their degree. When he got close to the English literature group, I got on the floor and positioned myself as close as I could get to the podium so I could get a good picture of her being handed the degree. It was a thrill for me when the chancellor called out, "June Hazel Burns, English literature, cum laude." A ripple of applause went up recognizing June's high achievement. Just as she was handed the degree, I snapped her picture, and as she started off of the stage and was coming toward me, I snapped more pictures of her.

As June was nearing me, I said, in a loud voice, "Yo, June, you did it!" June literally fell into my arms and we embraced. I said to her, "Sweetheart, from the first day I met you, I was hoping that, through everything, this day would come and now you have made it happen. My dreams for you have come true."

As we embraced, June blurted out, "That's not all, Jay. I didn't tell you earlier, but I got an email from KU this morning and I have been accepted into their graduate program to study for my master's degree."

"Sweetheart, that's tremendous news. Your dreams and my dreams are the same, and your dreams are now coming true. We are still together, so that makes me the luckiest guy on the planet."

CPSIA information can be obtained
at www.ICGtesting.com
Printed in the USA
LVHW041640230523
747801LV00020B/355